TENDER COURAGE

TENDER COURAGE

A Reflection on the Life and Spirit of Catherine McAuley
First Sister of Mercy

By

M. Joanna Regan, RSM
and
Isabelle Keiss, RSM

Franciscan Herald Press
1434 West 51st Street
Chicago, Illinois 60609

Library of Congress Cataloging-in-Publication Data

Regan, M. Joanna (Mary Joanna)
    Tender courage.
    Includes endnotes, bibliography, and index.
    1. McAuley, Catherine, 1786-1841. 2. Sisters of Mercy
—Biography. 3. Nuns—Ireland—Biography. I. Keiss,
Isabelle. II. Title.
BX4483.8.R44 1988   271'.92'024 [B]   87-30483
ISBN 0-8199-0197-3

MADE IN THE UNITED STATES OF AMERICA

CONTENTS

Contents

Forward

Responding to the urging in *The Documents of Vatican II* that religious institutes pursue the adaptation of religious life and customs to meet the needs of the Church in this age, not only through reflection on the Gospels but also with regard to the particular spirit and mission of the foundress, the Federation of the Sisters of Mercy of the Americas commissioned a reflective study of the life and works of Catherine McAuley in an effort to interpret her charisma and its implications for the world of today.

Sparse memoirs of companions, an oral tradition of her sayings, and a few notebooks recording novices' notes on Catherine McAuley's retreat instructions and comments on the Rule, give some insight to the worldwide phenomenon of the spirit that has marked Sisters of Mercy for more than 150 years, even though separated by time, geography, and social conditioning and by structures that made new foundations independent of one another. However, for insight into the person, the woman who gave to the Institute of the Sisters of Mercy its spirit and charism, the preeminent source is some 200 extant letters[1] which speak to Sisters of Mercy today, energizing them with a vitality faithful to the charism transmitted from generation to generation.

Rapid expansion of the institute provided the impetus for letter-writing. The letters, treasured and preserved by their recipients, provide direct knowledge of the character and personality of the author, and filter those influences which streamed through her consciousness, shaping the fledgling Institute of the Sisters of Mercy into what would become the largest congregation in the world established by an English-speaking Catholic.

In allowing her to speak for herself, the letters of Catherine McAuley give an immediacy and a personal slant that make events and observations extraordinarily vivid. Whether the letters are charting her response to the people in her life, the events of her time, her expectations, debate, disappointment, or delight, they allow us to see the wit, the loyalty, the passion, the compassion, the affection, of this woman of tender courage.

This book is neither a comprehensive biography nor a psychological analysis. It is a study of Catherine McAuley in an effort to have spirit touch spirit across two centuries to gain insight into her spirit and charism, to recapture her original vision so that new life develops. Its purpose is to picture the strong, tender, courageous woman in whom the vision became visible in the hope that the courage with which she approached the impossibilities of her time will animate us in our time to struggle for justice and peace with her spirit.

Social and political events of Catherine McAuley's times are touched upon only lightly since several well-documented works, primarily *Catherine McAuley* by R. Burke Savage, SJ, *Mercy Unto Thousands* by Sister M. Bertrand Degnan, RSM, and most recently, the data collected by Sister Angela Bolster, RSM, for the *Report of the Historical Commission on the Cause of Catherine McAuley* give extensive biographical analysis.

Catherine McAuley's charism, a gift of the Spirit, accentuated in her a deep response to the mercy of God in Christ. The goal of this study is to explore the profound intention underlying the historically-conditioned expression of her vision of following the example of the Gospels in serving human needs so as to articulate that vision in the language of our time.

Catherine McAuley's apostolic entry was to the neediest, the poorest, the most miserable. And yet there was simultaneously a strategy of linking those people with the wealthy, the free, the more able, so that a collaborative relationship ensued, connecting the rich to the poor, the healthy to the sick, the educated and skilled to the uninstructed, the influential to those of no consequence, the powerful to the weak. In this light then, the mercy charism she embodied may be understood as the religious dimension of governance. As such it is intrinsically a social spirituality, not an individualistic one. Movement toward the neediest, the oppressed—in addition to its unquestionably personal focus—requires a sense of the whole, a social context.

The first two sections of this book are biographical, reflecting on the shaping influences of family, friends, and country, the eighteenth century Ireland into which Catherine McAuley was born. The third section, based primarily on analysis of the extant letters, explores Catherine McAuley's charism of mercy, her leadership and governance of the new institute, and the development of the mission, spirituality, and marvelous humanity of the first Sister of Mercy.

The major research for this book was accomplished by Sister M. Joanna Regan who was chosen by the governing board of the Federation of the Sisters of Mercy of the Americas to author this study. After working in the archives of the twelve original foundations in Ireland and England, as well as visiting those in the United States holding relevant materials, Sister Joanna shared her reflections in presentations to audiences of Sisters of Mercy throughout the United States, to various communities in Ireland, Belize, and to the Latin-American Conference which met in Honduras in 1981, in order to test her insights against the lived experience of Sisters of Mercy everywhere.

Sister Joanna's death from cancer prevented her completing this study, but its substance is the fruit of her inspiration, her insights, and her own untiring effort despite incapacitating illness to see it to completion.

Because of her collaborative style of exploring Catherine McAuley's spirit and charism, it is impossible to express gratitude to all who expanded her insights during this process. It is essential, however, to thank Sister M. Concilia Moran, past Administrator General of the Sisters of Mercy of the Union, whose proposal initiated this study; Sister M. Silverius Shields, past executive director of the Federation of the Sisters of Mercy who fostered Sister Joanna's research in innumerable ways; and the archivists and researchers in Mercy communities around the world who so generously assisted the investigation.

My own deep gratitude for a friendship rich and rare is "...still appreciation/Out of plumb of speech."[2] For the sabbatical leave from Gwynedd-Mercy College to complete this work, I am indebted to my community, the Sisters of Mercy of Merion, Pa. To the University of Notre Dame, I am grateful for affording me, in an appointment as visiting scholar in the English Department during 1986-1987, an academic atmosphere of friendship, care, and encouragement in which to work.

June 1987   Isabelle Keiss, RSM

Part One

SHAPING INFLUENCES

Chapter I

FAMILY AND COUNTRY

Why is it that one child in a family, a neighborhood, a national environment will stand taller in dedication, personal integrity, freedom of spirit, and ability to transcend the difficulties of life?

Only when all secrets are unlocked will sure knowledge be available as to why those who could say YES to life—to its humiliations, incompleteness, inconsistencies, injustices, traumas, and pain as well as its joys, blessings, goodness, truth, and beauty—become free, happy, whole persons able to bestow themselves where they will and able to free others from self-imposed imprisonments.

The gifted, freed, self-possessed woman Catherine McAuley accomplished what she did by faithful response to the call of God as she heard it in each moment of her life. In the paradox which is the Christian life, her free and active responses to joy and sorrow unshackled her spirit, giving her personal liberty in the midst of constraints, a freedom which expressed itself in compassionate and tender regard for all whose lives she touched.

It began some 200 years ago. One small child's heart stirred with pity for those who were poor. These stirrings grew strong and deep. Mercy, "misericordia"—bringing one's heart to misery, to wretchedness—shaped the core of the developing child into the woman of compassion, Catherine McAuley, an heiress who would give all her wealth to the poor, and a woman of faith who would give to the Church a new religious family.

Born in 1778,[3] Catherine grew from child to woman during those tumultuous times when emergent awareness of human dignity and responsibility created resistance to kings, a new sense of individual rights, and a growing belief in the perfectability of human persons. Both acceptance of and resistance to the ideas spawned or fomented in the American and French Revolutions, along with bitter differences concerning religious faith bred the seething tensions of the Ireland of her day.

Catherine's father, James McGauley,[4] had won back some of the wealth lost to his ancestral family by the imposition of the Penal Code.[5] Designed to break the power of wealthy Irish Catholic families, the Code forced Roman Catholics to subdivide their holdings equally among all their children. In practice this soon reduced strong influential families to poverty and inconsequence. But James McGauley had developed an artisan's skill at carpentry and found himself in much demand while Georgian Dublin was being built in classic, restrained architecture. His ability to grasp opportunities led him to wealth and a measure of influence as he progressed from carpenter to contractor to grazier to gentleman. As historical records show, he signed himself on leases registered during the twenty-five years previous to Catherine's birth.

James married Elinor Conway, a young woman thirty years his junior who had been raised in a wealthy Catholic professional family. Very much influenced by the social mores of Protestant Anglo-Irish[6] Dublin, Elinor belonged to the thinking of the drawing rooms and salons of her times. Not disposed toward conventional Catholic practices, she "considered liberty of conscience so essential that she thought constraint or the obligation of performing any duties of religion foreign to its spirit."[7] From her Catherine inherited this independent mind and was never easily shaken from her convictions even when persons of wealth and greater influence stood against her.

Elinor formed her three children—Catherine, Mary, and James—in a code of conventional manners and moral integrity that required much self-imposed discipline. Catherine, from that training, acquired an enviable self possession and grace that won her admiration from high and low throughout her lifetime. She would eventually not only flawlessly receive members of the Court of St. James at the new Bermondsey convent in London, but also put boatmen of Dublin's Canal Barge at their ease in her presence when she "took tea with the men" during her foundation travels in Ireland.

Under the watchful eyes of her charming young mother, and older, greathearted father, Catherine learned both to conduct herself with the delicate good manners of polite society and to share the blessings of wealth with the poor. These inherited complementary traits created a rich composite in her personality.

Although it was not a common proclivity in the cities and fashionable circles to value poor children, Catherine observed a kind father in his fifties gathering the poor Irish children of the lanes and byways near their great-house, Stormanstown, despite the protests of his beautiful and brilliant wife who disliked what she considered the vulgar associations connected with his work among the poor. Even though her father died when she was but five years old, remembrance of his care and concern for those children and of his carefully instructing them in their faith expanded Catherine's generous impulses and turned her outward toward others throughout her life. Observation of his efforts prepared her to appreciate the necessity of educating the poor and inculcating in them a desire to advance themselves.

After the death of her husband, Elinor carried out her promise to have the children receive their First Holy Communion and confirmation in the religion in which they had been baptized, but under the pressure of such considerations as the temporal welfare of her children, and the personal solicitations of influential Protestant friends, she lapsed into virtual apostasy and did not attend to her children's practice of the Roman Catholic faith. Her intense anguish on her deathbed allows the conjecture that she may have felt remorse at this neglect.

The scene Catherine experienced during her mother's last illness and death caused her to fear death for much of her adult life. Only after she had witnessed so many of the poor die peacefully and observed many sisters yield themselves easily to God with evident happiness were her fears erased.

Events, sights, and sounds of her native city also shaped Catherine's response to life. Dublin had grown prosperous and throbbed with national pride during her youth and adolescence. Her native city had successfully created an aesthetic vista of stately public buildings and elegant neighborhoods with grand Georgian houses built around lovely green squares or parks. Dublin also had succeeded in asserting the rights of the Irish Parliament to exercise for Ireland the same powers as the English Parliament exercised for England. Irish nationalism encompassed renewed loyalty to King George III as King of Ireland and head of Ireland's Parliament[8] along with agitation for an independent Ireland.

The sense of nationalism alive in the world of her childhood and adolescent years never left Catherine. Writing later in letters sent back to Dublin from England and from foundations in various parts of Ireland, Catherine revealed the sense of Irish identity that those times had cut into her.

The seething tensions of the times saw the loss of the American Colonies by England and the emergence of the Republic of France, the Republic that beheaded its king, queen, and members of its nobility, as well as anyone suspected of non-agreement with those in power. This turmoil made it impossible for England's ruling party to allow her new partner country to grow strong or wealthy. Adverse effects of the reign of terror resulted in government leaders being determined to hold down the dispossessed, the discontented, and the disfranchised.

While it cannot be known precisely what Catherine knew of the call for liberty, equality, fraternity, or of the Declaration of Independence's assertion that all men are created equal and entitled to life, liberty, and the pursuit of happiness, it is likely that she heard them discussed and vehemently argued. She herself imbibed a fully democratic spirit. Believing in liberty of action for herself, she easily granted it to others, and tried to create a classless society among her first associates. She did this in spite of the fact that the strictly hierarchical world in which she lived—the world portrayed by Dickens, Austin, Thackery, and the Bronte sisters—was too often cold, harsh, self-righteous, and merciless to those considered inferior—the poor, the sick, or the handicapped. Those who suffered the hardships of poverty were blamed for it as being improvident, lazy, or morally degenerate. Little pity or kindness was offered and those who received charity were made to feel their subservience. Charity, salted and peppered or coated with humiliations, was fed to the poor as a matter of course.

In this very world, a young Catherine McAuley recognized that the poor needed shelter, education, health care, and jobs. She somehow understood that most poor were not responsible for their own misery. As she looked at the realities, she determined to do what she could to relieve suffering and to build new possibilities for others, revealing both her father's and her mother's strong imprint upon her shaping in a 19th century environment that did not expect independent action by its women, much less creative initiatives.

Although in the fifteen years following the death of James McGauley, Elinor and her children had their residence in a fashionable section of Dublin rather than in the suburban mansion, Stormanstown, their standard of living remained one of affluence. Records of transactions in the sale of property in 1784, 1789, 1790, and 1796[9] suggest that this income allowed Elinor to support the social life style to which she had been accustomed.

Since the property sold in 1796 was apparently her last holding, and historic accounts suggest that Elinor McAuley endured a long illness before her death, it is likely that she spent her last years residing in her physician brother's home. That Catherine was with her at her death is certain. It is also plausible that Catherine first learned, in caring for her mother, the skills that she would employ so devotedly toward countless sick.

After Elinor's death whatever money or property was left was invested in the Company of Apothecaries,[10] with William Armstrong, a distant relative and an official of the company, entrusted with managing the finances for the McAuley children.[11]

Chapter II
AN IRISH CATHOLIC

After the death of her mother, Catherine began to take a firm grip on her Roman Catholicism. Residing with her Conway relatives provided Catherine with firsthand experience of living in a thoroughly Catholic environment. Accompanying Anne Conway on errands of charity recalled to her the devotion to the poor she had observed in her father. There in the crowded lanes of Dublin, she first heard the cries of starving children and of those in pain and fever as she went on visits of charity with her cousin. These cries haunted her dreams, waking her in the night for years to come. She longed to respond as she longed to remain with the Conways. But her respite there was short lived.

A personal experience of actual poverty brought on by an abrupt reversal of Dr. Conway's fortunes heightened her appreciation of the plight of the poor. It was an experience in which hunger and cold invaded the daily life of the household to the degree that whole days were spent without food, and furniture was sold to meet creditors' demands.

Her personal income too small to be of help to the Conway family, to relieve the burden on them she accepted the invitation to join the Armstrong household where her sister and brother had lived since Elinor McAuley's death. Catherine was aware that she was a woman of negligible financial resources. Without living the life style of the poor, she knew the embarrassment and humiliation of being a poor relative.

The vehemence of the times descended on Catherine in the Armstrong household in hostility to her adherence to her Roman Catholic faith.[12] It was an atmosphere where the Roman Church, its pope, bishops, and priests were blamed for every fault and deficiency of the Irish peasant. Blind to the economic system that made the poor poorer, many thought in good faith that if they could wrest the Irish poor from their oppressive Church, their moral character and their living standards would improve. That tithes to support the Anglo-Catholic Church added to the oppression of poor farmers was lost on those who formed opinions from untested assumptions or inherited bigotry. Without investigation it was assumed and often asserted that the popish Church kept the native population indigent, dishonest, irresponsible and, most dangerous of all, traitorous—willing in their allegiance to a foreign "Roman" ruler to ally themselves with Spanish or French to bring ruin upon the Protestant gentry of Ireland and gain access to England for its enemies.

When Catherine came to the Armstrongs, fear of loss of privilege and change in the order of things occasioned by the Act of Union and the consequent dissolution of the Irish Parliament had heightened hostilities between Catholics and Protestants. Once fears are aroused, exaggerated stances follow naturally. Every evil is easily attributed to those to whom one is opposed, as is every good easily attributed to those with whom one stands. So it was in the Armstrong household where Catherine met men and women whose honor and integrity demanded that they despise Papists. Ignorant of the true conditions of the Irish, overlooking the deep social injustices at work in Ireland, these Protestants were totally unaware that the abject misery of the people was not of their own doing, but the result of decades of degradation forced upon them by laws that protected privilege and penalized defenselessness.

While many of the Anglo-Irish landed aristocracy, church leaders, and professionals—those in control of the best lands as well as the political, social, and economic processes—agreed that the Irish should have a measure of freedom, they also concurred that the Irish must be subjugated and controlled for their own good. While they disagreed about how much control was proper, few Anglo-Irish thought of Ireland's belonging to the Irish any more than contemporary Americans thought of the United States as belonging to the Native American tribes.

The Irish people over whom the argument arose had a natural courtesy, an irrepressible humor, a primitive realism imbued with faith and trust in God's looking after them that enabled them to develop survival tactics to endure and prevail as a people.

Since paradox is the stuff of life, there is rarely a victory in which there is no defeat. Irish survival tactics weakened some of their most generous and noble sentiments. As a people, many became hidden rather than reserved, crafty more than cautious, equivocal rather than straight forward, flatterers and exploiters of native charm more than spontaneous, and eventually, betrayers of one another for food, a piece of land, a job. At the same time, the paradox was full-blown, for they could starve themselves to feed another, open-heartedly put themselves at another's service—a prey to exploitation—and be simple, direct, fun loving, merry, and spontaneous as children whenever they acted out of the native giftedness of a deep and ancient heritage.

Temptation exists in every age to dehumanize those considered enemy with a name that permits objectifying or sub-humanizing them. Inhumanity visited upon Papists masqueraded often as virtue. The annals of events in Ireland recorded in journals and daily papers during the 18th and early 19th centuries testify that the abiding sense of injustice, of being despoiled, humiliated, and betrayed that still exists has roots deep in history—roots that can be destroyed only by reconciliation through forgiveness on all sides.

A lived rather than articulated awareness of this need for unity among peoples shone in Catherine McAuley who knew and appreciated Irish, Anglo-Irish, and English who entered her life. Radiant in her was the best of the Irish heritage with its willing self-sacrifice and its joyful zest for life. But she did not come upon her heritage easily. She became a woman stretched upon the hard wood of the cross of her times, suffering with others its agonies, injustices, and misunderstandings.

Catherine's womanhood began in the aura of popular expectation of great blessings to come from the union of England and Ireland. Repeal of the Penal Laws was expected to be completed as well as a greater enfranchisement of the Irish. But the Union of 1800[13] provided only a step-sister relationship to Ireland and its Irish peasantry.

Full family membership was granted only to Anglo-Irish and eventually to Scots-Irish. Lines between privileged and non-privileged were again drawn more tightly. Privileged groups foresaw loss of privilege, loss of ability to control the destiny of Ireland and the potential loss of their own fortunes and holdings against the upsurge of the Irish Roman Catholic majority who constituted four-fifths of the population. Protestant Ireland therefore resisted strenuously the Emancipation Movement led by the genius of Daniel O'Connell. With the Union's galvanizing new hostilities, resentments, and violent reactions, Catholic emancipation was not to come until 1832.

Around 1800 when Catherine moved into the Armstrong household, she personally encountered in her cousin's home the explicit attitude that Roman Catholic Irish were ignorant, willful, wrong-headed enemies of the Crown and of all common decency. Any report of uprising or atrocity perpetrated by the Irish people was broadcast throughout Anglo-Irish circles, heating to great flames of moral indignation and self congratulation the righteousness of their opinions that Irish Papists possessed an inferior humanity.

Because of the rapid growth of the Irish population, shortage of land put the rural Irish poor in bitter competition with one another for land, and decline of industry in cities created massive unemployment. With more persons than space, rents rose to destructive heights. Interest on money borrowed to sow grain wiped out any profit from hard labor. Improvements made in cottages forced up the rent. Whoever could not pay was evicted to give his place to another waiting to get a piece of land to feed his family. The homeless were forced thereby either to dig out space in bogs, plaiting wild thorn-bush to create a makeshift roof, or to wander about as beggars—a terrible fate for the proud Irish.

Fish, wild fowl, game of enclosed estates were forbidden to the poor, even to the starving. Anyone caught poaching could be maimed, hanged, or transported. But none of these things was alluded to among the Dublin great houses where Catherine lived, a self-possessed young woman. She faced hostile and vigorous attacks on her religion whenever some new account of a riot or burning of a great house was reported. Catherine, having had firsthand contact with the desperate poverty of the urban poor during the visits of charity undertaken with her cousin before she joined the Armstrong household, kept her peace and her convictions. She would give up neither her religious faith nor her belief in the potential of the Irish poor.

It continued, however, to be a real affront to William Armstrong that Catherine would not accept Protestantism. He could hope to settle with a good husband a woman who was Protestant. Since this was his responsibility toward a woman under his protection, he felt he could not carry out his duty to her while she remained Roman Catholic. Regularly with sister, brother, cousins, friends, the argument began: why are you so stubbornly committed to the Church of the ignorant, the peasant, the drunkard, the traitor?

In this environment where anti-Roman Catholic prejudice constituted the social ambience, Catherine quietly refused to yield her faith to the appeals of devoted Protestant relatives and friends who sought to attend to her best interests. In a land where the word Irish was an Anglo-Irish denigration, where the Irish were thought worthless and impossible to change, Catherine held her Irish heritage proudly. In a land where Irish Roman Catholics experienced a denial of their citizenship rights and third-class status, she held her faith tenaciously, experiencing it as the bedrock of her identity.

The non-Catholics among whom Catherine was reared were persons of conspicuous integrity whereas, on every side of her the repellent vices of intemperance and general disorderliness seemed to bear sorry evidence against the religion she had inherited. Perceiving the Protestants close to her as people of virtue and high principle, Catherine, troubled at their contempt for everything Catholic, determined to investigate the Protestant position in an effort to understand, and if possible, accept their views. Her reading, however, while it did not convince her, left her disturbed with her inability to refute the errors she sensed it contained. Catherine both loved and admired her relatives and Protestant friends. She would have chosen to be one in sentiment and practice with them if to do so had been conscientiously admissible. To remain resolute under attack without aggressiveness, to endure deep hurt without bitterness, to continue to hold in affection those who opposed and criticized what she so loved, pointed to rich gifts of the Spirit at work in her understanding love and tender courage.

Out of this tangled religious experience, Catherine knew that she had discerned her possession of the gift of faith and recognized that she could not be separated from it. But she also recognized that her faith had been nurtured with devotions learned in childhood, rather than by understanding gleaned from mature study of Scripture and doctrine. Her faith under attack, she experienced the lack of formal knowledge needed to know where the attack was in error. This shaking experience led to her resolve to educate herself further and enkindled the determination to do whatever she could do to educate the poor in the truths of their faith. It would also lead her to form valuable friendships with learned priests whose influence would be far-reaching.

Catherine brought to her life at the Armstrongs the compassion bequeathed by her father and the independence of mind bequeathed by her mother. Her father's religious fervor crossed with her mother's intellectual independence; her mother's gentility and ability to associate in society crossed with her father's identification and involvement with the poor, the outcast, and the downtrodden to rearrange themselves finely mixed in Catherine. She arrived at the Armstrongs with the gifts her parents had bestowed, developed, and embedded in a tender courage of her own, able to identify with her faith and her heritage with dignity, grace, and charm.

Chapter III

"HIDDEN LIFE" IN A QUAKER HOUSEHOLD

Among the visitors to the Armstrongs was William Callaghan, a distinguished chemist, and like William Armstrong, prominent in teaching and administration at Apothecaries' Hall. After a long sojourn in India, William Callaghan had brought a chronically ill wife back to the often harsh, cold, damp climate of Ireland. Coming to know Catherine in frequent visits to the Armstrongs and charmed by her grace and abilities, this childless couple, well past the stage to attempt to bring up a small child, asked the self-possessed young woman to be a daughter to them. Grateful for this opportunity to provide for herself, Catherine accepted the Callaghan offer.

The Callaghan's Coolock Estate was a Quaker household, an atmosphere tolerant of differing religious faiths. William Callaghan, nominally a member of the Established Church, rarely attended any worship; his wife, Catherine, a gentle Quakeress, set the tone in which affirmation of the indwelling Spirit and redemptive love were spiritual realities. Love of God and love of neighbor found expression in social attitudes and concerns, in service, and in education. The Friends' belief that there is potential for good in each person and the consequent sensitivity to human degradation, ignorance, suffering, and injustice touched a responsive chord in Catherine.

Joining their household in 1803, Catherine remained with them for twenty years, years which may be termed her "hidden life" in which she not only developed spiritually, but also learned the management of a large estate. William Callaghan watched Catherine take over the management of the household for his sick wife, and, in great demand as a lecturer, began to entrust many of the other duties of his twenty-two acre estate to her. Entrusted also with the distribution of their alms to the poor, Catherine often amazed Mr. Callaghan by her ability to handle money, stretching it so as to serve multiple purposes of mind, heart, and body.

Particularly important in the shaping of Catherine McAuley was the Quaker respect and appreciation for the talents of women. Their pioneering acknowledgement of the spiritual equality of men and women liberated Quaker women to share both religious and secular responsibilities. It seems probable that awareness that the Quaker "Women's Meetings" were charged with particular concern for the poor of their own sex planted seeds deep in Catherine's soul, seeds which would blossom in her oft-quoted maxim: "Nothing is more productive of good to society than the careful instruction of women."

Catherine's services for the Callaghans allowed her to feel her own sense of dignity and worth, and led her to make a valiant effort to develop that same sense in others. She seemed to understand the assault it is on the human personality to be totally at the mercy of another's good nature, and utilized the funds available to her not only to relieve needs but also to foster the dignity of the poor receiver.

Gathering young girls she found loitering in the neighborhood who had no employment and no skills to recommend themselves for jobs, Catherine taught them needlework and domestic skills, and after they had acquired some facility, opened a shop to sell their needlework. Family, friends, and visitors to the Coolock Estate quickly patronized the "shop," and Catherine was soon able to expand her classes and to pay the learners for their products.

As she developed a deeper understanding of her faith, Catherine's spirituality grew, fed both by reading matter supplied by priest mentors[14] and by daily hidden self-yielding to God. So skillful was she in keeping her religious practice out of public view that few who lived with her knew that she kept days of fast or abstinence. Even fewer knew the cost to her to suppress the joy and peace she found in her faith, nor the pain she experienced to hear it denigrated.

Devoted to the interests and care of the Callaghans, Catherine developed a profound affection for them and they for her. She wanted for them the faith that inspired and motivated her daily life. Long hours of attendance in Mrs. Callaghan's sick room afforded Catherine opportunity for ever-deepening reflection on the gospel, enabling her to find it a blueprint for action. Absorbing the style of response of Jesus of Nazareth, she found it a style to be imitated in every least detail. Catherine's early disciplined training gave her the background, the natural ability to present herself mildly, gently, and kindly. Her absorption in the life of Christ gave dimension, gentleness, charm to her self-possession.

She was to spend much time nursing Mrs. Callaghan through prolonged illnesses, learning many skills concerning the proper care of the sick from both visiting physicians and Mr. Callaghan who lectured at Apothecaries Hall on herbal medicines. It was the custom of the time that doctors taught a trusted member of the household both the treatments to be given to a patient and the symptoms to watch for and report.

Catherine's spiritual strength was experienced by those around her. She knew she exerted influence over others but hardly knew how much her very being affected them. Her desires were so intense that each of the Callaghans in turn, although they died a few years apart, responded to the genuine concerns Catherine expressed when answering questions about the source of the anxiety they felt in her. Although Mrs. Callaghan, who died in 1819, asked to have a priest instruct her, she required that Catherine never tell Mr. Callaghan lest he later disinherit her.

When William Callaghan knew that his own death was approaching, he soothed Catherine's fears concerning him, declaring that if it were her religion that made her the way she was, he really should investigate it. His instructions completed, Mr. Callaghan was received into the Church a few days before he died.

Catherine experienced the power of God's mercy at work in her desperate concern for both Catherine and William Callaghan at each one's approaching death. She had wanted with all the force of her being to share her faith with them. She learned in an incontrovertible way that it is genuine solicitude, genuine being—with another that moves hearts. As she made what she considered the Callaghans' best good her deepest concern, they each felt the reality of her compassion, of her desires for them, of her suffering for a faith they had not experienced as a loss except through her pain for them.

During his illness, William Callaghan wrote a new will leaving the substance of his estate divided between Catherine and a young cousin of Mrs. Callaghan's also residing, along with her husband, at the Callaghan estate. Overhearing a discussion under his window the same day he had signed the will, Mr. Callaghan requested that the lawyer attend him again, and added a codicil naming Catherine the sole residuary legatee of his entire estate. The cousin's young husband had spoken with some arrogance of how he would conduct the household when he was master, and intimated, among other things, that Catherine would be ousted.

The will contested, the court proceedings lasted more than a year. In the end, the codicil was upheld and Catherine declared sole heiress. A woman of strong feelings in her forties, she summoned up all she had learned about the management of estates, funds, great houses, as well as about the needs of single women, of the poor and the sick, to carry out the stewardship of her inheritance. William Callaghan's recognition that she would do good with his wealth fueled her resolve to find productive ways to serve the poor and unprotected.

Recognizing that one could give handouts week after week only to find the same poverty, the same indigence, the same inability of the poor to help themselves, the same no-exit life, she determined to use her inheritance to offset the causes of poverty, sickness, and ignorance and to remedy these evils in a systemic manner. The evil effects of harsh, unrelenting poverty, of debilitating sickness, and of crass ignorance of the simplest of life's processes she knew to produce the defeated human spirit, demoralized responses, and contagious self-hatred. She knew also that materially improved life was incomplete and unfulfilling without a corresponding growth in knowledge and love of God.

With these understandings carved deep in her heart, she took her desires and practical designs to confidants[15] who greatly favored her plan to build a property in Dublin that would provide a home for unprotected women and orphans, a schoolroom for poor children, and quarters for her and for those who would choose to work with her in attending Dublin's sick poor in their impoverished dwellings.

Part Two

HEIRESS AND STEWARD

Chapter IV

"KITTY'S FOLLY": AN IMPOSSIBLE SCHEME?

Shaped by her family, her times, and her circumstances, Catherine McAuley, with her bequest secured and plans well laid for a property on Lower Baggot Street,[16] employed architect and builder to create the headquarters for the work she envisioned, the personal investment of her life and fortune in the daily care of the poor, the sick, the unlettered, the unskilled, the handicapped, the castoffs of society.

With a multi-purpose design to accommodate several large schoolrooms, dormitories for unprotected working girls, an oratory, and private lodgings for herself and for the associates who would wish to aid in serving the poor, the house was established in a fashionable neighborhood where it also would become both the base from which Catherine and her associates visited the sick poor in their homes and in hospitals, and an employment agency for girls desiring positions in the homes of the wealthy.

Convinced that long-term improvement of the condition of the poor depended on education of the young, Catherine had planned from the beginning that the House of Mercy have space for a school. To prepare for this, during the three years when the Baggot Street property was under construction, she studied teaching methods. In an age of apprenticeships where observation and practice formed a large part of such training, Catherine became a regular instructor at St. Mary's Poor School,[17] traveled to France to observe teaching methods there, and visited the Kildare Place Society schools around Dublin.[18]

Catherine knew her society. She knew that living with Protestant relatives caused her to be identified as a Protestant. This gave her entree to Protestant schools and hospitals to learn their methodologies and to offer her services.

Her investigations of the educational methodologies of the much praised Kildare Model School revealed to her that there was indeed much pressure put upon Catholic children to abandon the practices of their faith. She determined to offer an education second to none in an environment that fostered the development of the students' own religious faith.

Most schools in the early nineteenth century were government schools which aimed to offer an elementary education to every child in Ireland with the announced philosophy that no proselytizing should occur. But theory was not practice. To erase the notion in Ireland that different religious practice did not necessarily diminish allegiance to crown and parliament nor color national spirit proved somewhat impossible.

When the Baggot Street building was nearing completion, the serious illness of Mary Macauley required that Catherine preside over the management of her sister's household. It soon became apparent to Catherine, by now an experienced nurse, that Mary would not recover. Before her death, however, she had the joy of Mary's being reconciled with the religion of her childhood. Not wanting to displease her husband, she requested he not know, but entrusted her eldest daughter, Mary Teresa, with her secret.

After Mary's death, while Catherine was making her home at the Macauley residence, tending to the care of her five nieces and nephews, an incident occurred which highlights the intensity of feeling religious bigotry could reach. Dr. Macauley's esteem for his sister-in-law held only one reservation, the possibility that his children would be influenced by her toward the faith he despised.

William Macauley, a militant Protestant hostile in every way to Roman Catholicism, persisted in trying to talk Catherine out of her practice of such a faith. He was aghast as were most of her relatives and friends at how she was deploying her inheritance, referring to the house on Baggot Street as "Kitty's Folly." They felt she wasted her fortune on those who could never improve and would not be grateful for what she was doing.

Using any opportunity that presented itself to urge his children to dissociate themselves from what he perceived as superstitious practices, he chose one evening to remind them how grieved their mother would be, pointing out that she had rejected the faith into which she had been born. In the tension of the exchange between them, Catherine informed him quietly that Mary had died a Roman Catholic. Enraged, he raced from the room to find his military sword. Catherine fled and sought refuge for the night at the home of Dr. Cusack, a close friend, who admitted her without question.

William arrived the next morning, ashamed and repentant. Realizing the passionate violence that religion could call up, they agreed never again to discuss each other's beliefs.

Catherine had envisioned that other lay women would choose to join the work at Baggot Street, carrying out the various services for the poor.

In the spring of 1827, Anna Maria Doyle, who had experienced some desires to become a Presentation nun, saw the strange building under construction and inquired as to its purpose. When Miss Doyle learned the use intended, "a strong interior impulse"[19] along with the encouragement of elderly parents who hoped she would be able to attend them in their old age, urged her to "unite in Miss McAuley's design."[20] Even though she also learned that the building had been dubbed "Kitty's Folly" by those who decreed an excellent inheritance was being wasted on an impossible scheme, Miss Doyle was not daunted.

Impatient to live a life of service and aware that Catherine's responsibility for the Macauley household would not yet permit her to take up residence at Baggot Street, Miss Doyle urged that the formal opening take place as early as possible. With the assurance of the builders that the House would be sufficiently available by September 24, Catherine readily accepted her suggestion; and on the feast of Our Lady of Mercy, Anna Maria Doyle and Catherine Byrn,[21] both young women still in their teens, opened the House of Mercy. This act would prove prophetic of Catherine's profound conviction that the work transcended her individual ownership and that the charism gained life in its multiple expressions.

Chapter V

"THE ORIGINAL INTENTION"

Within months of its opening, the House of Mercy had begun to realize all the goals its founder had envisioned. The crowded school where "five hundred girls... daily experience[d] the blessing of religious instruction, and [were] practiced in various branches of industry"[22] the residence where "young tradeswomen... [were] invited... at night as their home," the employment agency whose services were in demand, the refuge where orphans were sheltered, the visitation of the poor sick in their homes and in hospitals, all were made possible by the increasing numbers of "ladies" attracted to join in the work of the Baggot Street house.

From the beginning of the House of Mercy in 1827, Catherine, always practical, sought associates and companions who would work with her in her efforts to relieve the miseries of the day.

> Ladies who prefer a conventual life, and are prevented embracing it from the nature of property or connections, may retire to this house. It is expected a gratuity will be given to create a fund for the school and an annual pension paid sufficient to meet the expenses a lady must incur.[23]

Writing to Father Francis L'Estrange, the Carmelite Prior, Catherine explained not only the requirements for association, but the nature and purpose of the work in which they engaged, as well as potential plans for the future.

> The objects which the charity at present embraces are the daily education of hundreds of

poor female children and the instruction of young women who sleep in the house.

Objects in view—superintendence of young women employed in the house, instruction and assisting the sick poor as may hereafter be approved.

Truly remarkable is the economy with which she set out the description of her work, her associates, and her plans for expanding the enterprise. The letter contains barely a hundred words and yet a complete picture emerges from this succinct, business-like presentation.

The same letter raises speculation as to whether Catherine was responding to requested information or to the gossip and rumors swirling about the new building on Baggot Street when she asserts:

With full approbation of His Grace the Archbishop, the institution in Baggot Street is to go on according to the original intention.

The placement of her house where the poor would be visible to the rich and where young women could find employment nearby was deliberate. At the House of Mercy, young hopefuls were trained in needlework, laundry, and other domestic services. Success attended their efforts and it soon became one of the busiest and most called upon employment agencies in Dublin.

Having experienced the rich humanity of the poor she had visited in cottages, huts, and classrooms, Catherine knew them not as barbarians but as victims with many deficiencies to be addressed. She also knew that the rich, lacking the experiences which she had had that helped her to understand the poor, were victims of false assumptions and inherited prejudices. Desiring to connect the two groups to their mutual advantage, Catherine and her associates prepared unlettered and untrained young women with skills which enabled them to value themselves and to be valued in turn.

Convinced that the careful education of women contributed to incalculable good not only to them but also to society, Catherine saw that instruction in faith and its practice and training in good manners were also provided in order to lay a solid foundation for the day these young women would preside over hearths of their own. She knew what her society had to say of the Irish poor. In her mission of service, she wanted to provide means for unprotected girls and women to develop beyond that criticism.

The House of Mercy not only trained young women, but also provided a haven for those with employment who often had no safe place to live. Catherine's previous experience at Coolock of finding herself impotent to help such a person fueled her resolve to meet this need of the young women crowding Dublin in search of employment. She further resolved that appeals for admittance would be decided by those managing the House of Mercy, not sanctioned as the prerogative of a ladies' committee of benefactors of high social standing who met at intervals. Such a committee had refused her when she sought admission for a girl from the Coolock neighborhood to a residence managed by the Sisters of Charity.

In an age when the use of antisepsis, anesthesia, or antibiotics was unknown, death came early to those stricken with serious illness. Catherine knew that many deaths resulted from poor care especially among those who had no access to doctors and were ignorant of even simple methods of prevention and cure. To address this evil, she insisted upon daily visits to the sick poor in their homes. Catherine's ambition in her ministrations was to restore health as well as to comfort the sick and the dying. Visitation of the hospitals was begun when she realized that few priests ever had an opportunity to minister to the sick in even the most altruistic private doctor's hospital.

To tend sickness in wealthy homes, a doctor required someone from the household to carry out his instruction exactly, reporting the patient's progress. Catherine had for years experienced the role of trusted assistant to doctors as she nursed Mrs. Callaghan and the cottagers dependent upon the Callaghans, learning through these responsibilities how to care for many illnesses. While gifted to minister to spiritual and mental anguish, she also had the confidence of her patients, rich and poor, that her nursing skills were of the highest order. Both groups depended upon her for direction and good care. Her access to professional direction from close connection to the medical profession in her brother, brother-in-law, uncle, and protector enabled her to bring both healing and instruction to the sick.

The courtesy imbedded in Catherine shone in the specific environment of the Irish poor. She could enter scenes of abject misery with a cultivated courtesy that saw only the person. In scenes of wretched poverty and noisome illness, it was not in her to draw back involuntarily, avert her eyes, nor stiffen so as not to faint, her psyche long since won to the task of loving service. Her courtesy sustained through the perfect control she had of her body, her very presence expressed her compassion.

Catherine's demanding education by her mother, polished and proved during her Armstrong and Callaghan days, gave her a command of self similar to the dancer's control. In competition only with self, a dancer undergoes a rigorous discipline to command an inner directed response to the shape and build of rhythm and music. This absolute dedication will enable the dancer to release the divine within the self in dance. Those who achieve such artistry reveal gifts unsuspected.

With impeccable manners, Catherine McAuley could take the highest rungs of the social stage with poise and confidence. She bent this control to the ministry of courteous presence, a presence that revealed the divine spirit alive in her services of charity and mercy. With disciplined skill, she allayed the fears of the poor, the sick, and the ignorant in scenes of misery and suffering. Her self possession held tight rein on natural inclinations to turn away, show revulsion, or grow faint. This woman who possessed herself could freely share the gifts of her life with others. She could do more. She could inspire others to act in the same generous and compassionate way.

Chapter VI

DILEMMA AND DECISION

The house where young women were prepared to find employment as domestics or as assistants to dressmakers, confectioners, or other shopkeepers, where children were given a sound education along with an education in faith, and where women of good will devoted their personal energies and fortunes to caring for young women, children and the poor sick was not perceived in a favorable light by everyone.

Well-to-do gentlewomen of the nineteenth century carried baskets of food to the poor and visited the sick in cottage and hospital. They performed these services from motivations that ranged from inspired Christian behavior, to a moral duty to the less fortunate, to a superficial outing of condescension. To perform ministrations according to the pattern found in the Gospels required love, concern, caring for the person and, for Catherine McAuley, allowing the pain she encountered to enter her own heart.

That the effort of the ladies at Baggot Street was a response to the call of the gospel, not a self-serving benevolence born of condescension, was evident in the way they lived lives of service. As their numbers increased, a routine of life had developed that greatly resembled a religious institute. They arose at the same time, prayed communally at morning and evening, adopted a simple dress, and in response to a request from Anne O'Grady who had spent a year at the Presentation Convent, even began to address each other lightheartedly as "Sister." Their coordinated practice of spiritual and corporal works of mercy within and outside the house reflected their unity of purpose and mutual faith.

Catherine had worked closely with the clergy and hierarchy as her plans crystallized, relating to Archbishop Murray as to her ecclesiastical superior. He represented for her the blessing of the Church upon her works; and with his approval she established the work as an expression of her faith, seeking his permission and blessing for each new avenue of service to the poor or sick. Even with this cultivated attitude of identifying with the Church, Catherine, "not as yet undeceived as to the uncatholic nature of her project,"[24] as an early associate described her, never thought of herself as founding a religious order of women. But then neither did Archbishop Murray.

To establish the House of Mercy firmly as a lay institution, and to ensure its stability for all who would join in its works, Catherine, in April 1829, had vested the property in a trust. The terms of the trust, explicitly placing the house under the control, management, and direction of the archbishop, provided that if "any Tribunal deem [the works] ... incapable of being carried into effect, ... the whole premises shall be conveyed to the archbishop for his sole and private use."[25]

In all his interactions with Catherine McAuley, Archbishop Murray dealt with her as with a lay woman who did charitable and needed works within his diocese. Many of the clergy of the Dublin area, however, took offense that Catherine's work was not under the Church in a more structured way. Convinced as they were that all women needed male protection of some kind, they could not imagine that independent, undirected women could do good for the Church since "the unlearned sex could do [nothing]! but mischief by trying to assist the clergy."[26]

In spite of this opposition, the works progressed well. Dublin families of wealth began to be much aware of the house on Baggot Street and of servants trained there. Developing a circle of adherents, benefactors, and protectors, while also attracting members from among the most cultivated young women of Dublin, the new bastion for the poor on Baggot Street created worthy enemies as well. As it grew in strength, defenders and patrons of the Sisters of Charity and the Sisters of the Presentation, seeing the House of Mercy as a threat, pounced upon the new rival as unauthorized, unorthodox, and officially unrecognized by the Roman Catholic Church. Their criticisms reached a climax the day the chapel was dedicated and the archbishop not only permitted it to be opened for public Masses but also permitted all money collected at Masses said there to be used to support its works of charity. Antagonism became explicit at the dinner provided afterwards. Archbishop Murray was distressed that he was thought not to have given enough attention to what had been developing at Baggot Street. Whatever in his manner or private words betrayed his annoyance, one of the priests present was prompted to call on Miss McAuley shortly after and state unequivocally that the archbishop desired her to hand over her property to the Sisters of Charity who would conduct a legitimate work of the Church.

Aware of the personal antagonism of the parish administrator, Catherine immediately wrote to Dr. Murray, assuring him that the house was his to dispose of, but requesting that she might continue to live at Baggot Street since she had closed all other retreats. Her letter brought a mystified Archbishop Murray to her door. Somewhat testily he explained that he had no desire for her good works to cease nor for her to vacate the property. However, he acknowledged his embarrassment before his clergy by the fact that all the accoutrements of religious life existed without any attempt to so designate it. Feeling pressured by his clergy, the archbishop was distant, reserved, and defensive about his position as responsible for religious groups within the diocese, insisting that they must either behave as ladies of their station with regard to dress and other social proprieties or they must assume the duties and obligations of formal religious life.

The archbishop left Catherine with a difficult dilemma. She could choose between two options, neither of which would accomplish the purpose to which she had dedicated her fortune and her life. Simply dressed women could care for the poor sick in their homes, instructing family members about ongoing care. Efficient, quiet, soft-spoken, they could also do whatever needed to be done for the household without proving an embarrassment to the poor, and thus were welcome in tiny, crowded, impoverished dwellings. But a "lady" was a burden in this environment. The social mores of the Irish called upon the poor to attend to a lady and her comfort, an attitude which had the effect of increasing the duress on the sick poor.

The other option Catherine found equally problematic. She feared that as religious they would be closed off from major works for the poor in which they were engaged. She considered the visitation of the sick poor in their needs, both physical and spiritual, an essential service. Therefore, it saddened her to think of the demise of these works by the imposition of cloistered convent walls. She probably knew well that the Sisters of Presentation had begun in the same manner, as lay women responding to the pressing needs of the poor who eventually were no longer permitted by the rules of cloister to carry on their mission of charity once they became a religious order."[27]

However, faced with the distrust with which so many pious people regarded the arrangements at the House of Mercy, and encouraged by her advisors who procured copies of various rules of religious orders for her review, Catherine and her associates investigated them to see which could most easily be adapted to their purposes. When this was done, the Rule of the Presentation Order was unanimously preferred. The possibility of establishing a religious congregation had been a "point... often... discussed with her associates, who were all in favor of it, but still [Catherine had shrunk] from deciding on it."[28]

Architects had produced a conventual-style building; carpenters had installed a grating in the chapel; a common life-style had developed. And yet, "the idea of a convent starting up of itself in this manner"[29] had not occurred to Dr. Murray—or to Catherine McAuley.

Distaste for the idea of convent life from perceptions acquired during long years within Protestant households was a reality for Catherine. As late as September 1828, she had reiterated her intention that the House of Mercy was "to go on according to the original intention,"[30] a society of pious secular ladies who would devote themselves to the relief of suffering and the instruction of the ignorant. They would retain liberty to leave when they no longer felt inclined to render such service.

Early-acquired prejudice along with her fear that canonical religious life with its tradition of enclosure would not permit the breadth of needed activities to continue had caused Catherine to hesitate.

In the investigation that preceded her decision, Arch-bishop Murray proposed to spare Catherine, a woman fifty-two years of age, the restraints of a novitiate among strangers. Anticipating both the personal cost to her and the detrimental effect her absence would have, when a wise, experienced, spiritual woman would leave highly motivated and idealistic fledglings on their own, he of-fered to send to Baggot Street two professed religious of the order whose Rule they would choose to adapt to their purpose. In this way Catherine would remain free to direct the management of the House of Mercy while at the same time, she and as many of her companions as were thought suitable, might serve a novitiate under these religious.

However, Catherine, despite her personal repugnance for what she knew of convent customs, in faith that God was leading her, chose the most direct and practical means to learn the dimensions that religious life would add to their mission of mercy. Permission was sought for her, Anna Maria Doyle, and Elizabeth Harley to make a novitiate with the Sisters of the Presentation.

Chapter VII

FIFTY-TWO-YEAR-OLD NOVICE

At the George's Hill Convent, Catherine was plunged into a novitiate of silence, Scripture study, meditation, prayer, into a world that enlarged awareness of God's presence and created desire for union.

But the spiritual dimension did not comprise the whole life of the novice. Manual chores, practice in disciplined control of the exterior, ascetical practices of humility and mortification rounded out the education. Nothing exterior was left unnoticed or uncommented upon. The training at the Presentation Convent, demanding and sometimes demeaning, had as its object to crush the "old Adam" of St. Paul's letters and to put on the new person formed in the likeness of Christ.

The superior who had received Catherine at the Presentation Convent had treated her with a certain degree of deference in consideration of her age and her position, past and future. Her successor a few months later "openly declared herself against differences and privileges," and "kept her in perpetual agitation by giving her to understand that they would receive her companions to profession at the end of the year and postpone hers, or even reject her altogether."[31]

Despite the difficulty of this exceptionally strenuous novitiate under religious who had reservations about the suitability of preparing those destined for a new congregation, Catherine demonstrated she had already acquired the spirituality to endure extreme humiliation and mortification as well as the strength to endure being cut off from Baggot Street where imprudence during her absence would bring on untimely deaths. Remembered as one of the most lighthearted at recreation, she had brought with her the independent mind, the self assurance, the way of possessing herself that belonged to Anglo-Irish society. Catherine appreciated the goodness of those who taught her and relished the contemplative peace that deepened her. She recognized that contemplation should develop in the active religious greater courage, generosity, and spirit of service to carry out her active life.

Anna Maria Doyle also brought with her the good breeding of Anglo-Irish society. But with it she brought along her Catholic convent boarding school experience with its sense of the mystique of religious life. Her earlier aspiration to enter the Presentation Convent disposed her to accept traditional ascetical practices uncritically. Later letters of Catherine would indicate her concern that Sister Mary Anne Doyle had a tendency to give undue emphasis to the contemplative dimension in a dichotomy Catherine did not accept.

Elizabeth Harley's understanding of religious life had little opportunity to influence the new congregation for she died shortly after she returned to Baggot Street. Experienced as a "perfect novice" while at Presentation, long hours of servile work in the damp cellars under the kitchens broke her delicate health. When Catherine remonstrated on her behalf, she was reminded that she was not yet in charge of her own community and was taking liberties not open to novices.

Rooted in the experience at George's Hill was a tension that has lasted into modern times, the temptation to give priority to contemplative practices over active works. Mary Anne Doyle and those who felt as she did were eager to take on varieties of ascetical practices, convinced they were required of "proper" religious. In Catherine's vision, it was not rigid forms but the will to give one's life as perfectly as possible to God which makes one holy. She valued the practices that helped develop a will so tuned.

Their profession as Sisters of Mercy according to the Rule of the Sisters of the Presentation contained a proviso for alteration later in order to incorporate officially the works that had already become part of the House of Mercy. With knowledge of sick and dying associates among those awaiting them at Baggot Street, Catherine and her companions did not even remain for breakfast at the Presentation Convent after the profession ceremony, a puzzling breach of courtesy.

Perhaps the mystery enshrouded in this apparent lapse calls attention to what is still the overriding claim on Sisters of Mercy: the compelling response to the sick, the suffering, and the needy.

Part Three

FOUNDRESS

Chapter VIII

CHARISM CRYSTALLIZES

Extant letters graphically depict Catherine as a warm, wise, and witty woman, intimately involved in the spread of the Institute of Mercy in both Ireland and England. The woman writing to keep all foundations abreast of one another is affectionate, tender, funny, graceful, confiding, wise. The woman of business is direct, concise, well-bred. The woman of the Church writing to bishops and priests is candid, cordial, obedient, and dignified. The woman who is Superior writing to censure is pained, sandwiching reproof between affectionate greetings and long newscasts to assure it is the deed not the doer that draws her ire.

Greatheartedness and practicality are rarely united in one. In Catherine, they were; they had to be. Her greatheartedness involved compassion, gentleness, magnanimity, vision, and future-orientation. Her practicality involved common sense, directness, objective management of resources, and ability to deal with immediate possibilities.

Catherine McAuley's response to a "marked Providential Guidance" was such that she could write eight years after the foundation of the Sisters of Mercy: "We were joined so fast that it became a matter of general wonder."[32] As word of the new institute and its work spread, invitations to establish foundations came pouring in at Baggot Street.

Catherine's letters reveal how engrossed she was in managing a spreading institute and giving all her energy and attention to those in whom she was forming the spirit and tradition of the new congregation. Deep bonds of affection linked member to member in the fledgling community. Because she travelled to each new foundation, stopping at previously established ones en route, she both carried messages and was in her person a link connecting house with house, person with person, new members everywhere with all members of the institute.

Religious ceremonies of profession, reception, and the blessing of new convents that reunited old friends and introduced new ones, along with the constant circulation of Catherine's letters built to phenomenal strength in ten short years the sense of belonging to the same tradition. No conscious strategy for creating affectionate ownership for the institute by all the members and by each foundation could have been more effective than Catherine's spontaneous letter-writing. With a natural talent for sustaining bonds among the members of the community, she had begun a correspondence soon after the foundation of Tullamore, the first outside of Dublin, that would develop into what she called her *Foundation Circulars*. They covered:

> reports on health —
>> Poor Sister Teresa Carton is very ill but not dangerously. Your 'old mother' coughing away, not up for two days, but in high spirits. Sr. M Clare's cough not gone — all the rest well.[33]

> comments on new members —
>> Our last addition is very pleasing and quite strong. She is equal to Sister M. Cecilia in music and just the size of Sister Margaret Marmion whose child she is.

> and relayed what Catherine had heard of the respective community —
>> Mr. O'Rafferty gives a good account of you all and hopes you will multiply fast.

While these *Foundation Circulars* to the "foreign powers"[34] were intended to link all convents of the institute in bonds of mutual affection and interest, they give insight into the woman who was Catherine McAuley through their spontaneous outpourings.

None of this letter-writing was idle gregariousness. Catherine took the message of the gospel quite literally, that all who gathered as his followers were to be united in love for God and for one another. The story of their visits, their interest in each foundation's development, their tender hospitality toward sick visitors seeking "change of air" is a record of their living the union and charity commanded by Jesus in the Gospels.

Drawing upon years spent learning to respond to gospel imperatives through prayer and reflection as well as developing spiritual strength through self-forgetfulness and self-discipline, Catherine had acquired the conviction that the life of Christ was to be imitated. She not only entered the Gospels; she internalized them. For her Jesus was model, a way to be, a way to live.

The gift of the Spirit to Catherine, her charism,[35] accentuated in her an awareness of the mercy of God in Christ Jesus: salvation in the giving—the gift that was needed, neither earned nor deserved. Her years of private study to substantiate the faith that was in her led her to understand that God, responding to the brokenness or imbalance of humankind, sent his Son to teach us how to be human, to show us the way. The Scriptures drew the blueprint in Jesus' response to the brokenness of the human condition: "Offer the wicked no resistance... Turn the other cheek... Go a second mile... Love your enemies... Pray for those who persecute you... Heal the sick, the lame, the blind. What I want is mercy, not sacrifice."

For a long time Catherine McAuley would not have been able to put the word on what she was about as "mercy." She discovered mercy at work in her life, experiencing within her concrete situation, her own need. Reflecting on these experiences, she found a sense of God's abiding presence.

Catherine had felt at the Conways what it was to be orphan, to be without any income of consequence, and finally when the Conway fortune vanished, what it was to be cold and hungry. At the Armstrongs she experienced what it was to be ignorant, without an educated intellectual support for the faith that was hers. At the Callaghans she learned what it was to have no home of her own to which she could bring women who needed protection. Deep reflection on moments of need, and awareness of having been rescued, lifted up, restored, became the spring-board of Catherine McAuley's loving outreach to others.

Her heart actively and lovingly imitated Jesus in his merciful response, showing tenderness toward all, especially the sick and the needy. The cries of poor, sick, starving children of Dublin's slum areas, which she first heard while accompanying Anne Conway on errands of charity, continued to awaken her from many comfortable beds until she opened the House of Mercy. At the Armstrongs, she had learned what prejudice, bigotry, and ignorance did to the thinking of honest, morally upright persons whom she cherished. At the Callaghans, tutored by physicians and pharmacists, she had learned through nursing Mrs. Callaghan through years of chronic illness and through tending sick cottagers of the Coolock estate in her name, the skills which would alleviate pain, restore health, or comfort the dying. As a volunteer teacher at St. Mary's Parish, she had learned how devoid of skills for ordinary life the poor were, and soon determined their needs to be skills and education, not handouts, temporary remedies, or lectures.

Awareness that her charism, her gift for others, was mercy began to be an explicit consciousness for Catherine when Anna Maria Doyle suggested opening the house on Baggot Street on the feast of Our Lady of Mercy, a piety with which Catherine, having lived in Protestant surroundings for most of her life, would not have been familiar.

As the plan became the House of Mercy, and subsequently the Institute of the Sisters of Mercy, she began to reflect on this distinguishing characteristic in letters, in verse, and in her writing of the Rule for the new institute.

As she compiled the Rule, Catherine's initial deviation from the Presentation text introduced an emphasis which reveals explicitly her particular spirituality: "Mercy, the principal path pointed out by Jesus Christ to those who are desirous of following Him."

Her absorption in the Word of God, written and incarnate, called her to imitate the example of Jesus in translating the love of God to others. In her experience of her own limitations, Catherine had found a God of love, a hidden God whose healing grace helped her transcend her frustrations, bitterness, and weaknesses and enabled her to translate her own pain into a deep compassion for others. In this compassion, she experienced the alleviating effect created by her willing entry into the pain of others.

Catherine somehow grasped intuitively that mercy is gift given in response to need, neither earned nor deserved. She did not shrink from the demands mercy places on whoever would extend it. She knew that rendering the merciful service was not an act of beneficence, but one of gratitude to God for mercy received.

Catherine McAuley could have been insulated and isolated against the miserable poverty of Dublin. Instead she recognized the call of the Spirit, and accepted it with a grateful love and a willingness to put it at the service of others. As recipient of God's mercy, she saw herself as steward. Gifts given were gifts for others. Direct and practical in her response, she went out into gutter and garret to teach, to sooth, and to shelter. She had discovered that her charism, her gift for others, was mercy, a charism to the cutting edge of brokenness or imbalance.

Giving outward expression to this inner grace, with a singularly keen eye for the special needs of her time and an astute perception of the methods by which they could be successfully met, she quickly attracted others drawn by a similar call to respond to the action of God in their lives.

Called by God to share life in this community of mercy, to be strengthened in bonds of union and charity to go out to reveal the love of the Father in service to the needy, Catherine and these first Sisters of Mercy cherished as the essence of the charism which they had received, the recognition and the fostering of the dignity of every human person. The poor they sought to serve were those in want, powerless, oppressed, or victimized, struggling daily to live in justice and equity. The sick they endeavored to restore were those in need of caring concern along with healing. The ignorant they desired to instruct were those whose need was knowledge both to live life productively and to experience the mysteries, the wonders of mind and spirit which contribute to a person's understanding of self and of God.

In responding to this call, the lives of Catherine and her Sisters of Mercy signaled so visibly compassion, forgiveness, and understanding, along with eager zeal for the coming in fullness of the Father's kingdom, that their multiplying members drew from Catherine the observation: "The fire that Christ cast upon them is kindling very fast."[36]

Chapter IX

LEADERSHIP AND GOVERNANCE

As word spread of the notable ability of each Convent of Mercy to relate the Christian message to its own particular locality by meeting manifold needs, more and more bishops pressed Catherine to establish foundations in their dioceses. With zeal equal to the invitations, Catherine took great joy in finding Baggot Street's daughter houses ready to follow its example in being "prepared to divide." The sharing of resources of personnel, money, and goods with a new foundation, while it put a burden on those remaining, was a burden that brought about a rich return: rapid increase of members, variety of talent for works of mercy discovered, and the lives of more and more people affected for good.

Study of the spread of the Institute of Mercy reveals a pattern. Made aware of the pain and suffering of others, Catherine McAuley, for whom the life of Jesus was normative, held herself open to requests and importunities on their behalf, took counsel to discern how best to effect relief and improvement, assessed financial and personnel resources, decided what to do, and set out with faith and trust in God to do it. Her extraordinary leadership qualities flowed from this confidence. With a clear vision of the mission to which she was called, Catherine used whatever influences would assist her, whatever resources she could obtain, in whatever form the needs of the poor and oppressed required.

Although the delineation of Catherine McAuley's role as foundress of the Sisters of Mercy—her leadership and governance of the young institute—breathes forth from her own pen in the extensive correspondence through which she animated each foundation, testimony to the

49

confidence which her early associates had in her leadership is explicit:

> The spirit of mercy and compassion for the poor which animated and, as it were consumed her, made her sometimes adopt plans for their relief which to some, appeared beyond the limits of prudence, but the success with which her undertakings were usually attended showed that she was guided by a heavenly wisdom.[37]

Catherine was not indiscriminate about agreeing to new foundations. She gave grave consideration to the possibilities both for giving personnel from Baggot Street and for the potential of financial support at the prospective location. A risk taker, she was neither imprudent nor improvident.

A careful provider, Catherine had practical good sense to evaluate conditions from which the sisters would best offer services to the poor. She wanted no luxuries, but she did want adequate shelter, adequate prayer and reflection space, and the confidence that there was adequate financial support.

When arranging to make a foundation, she negotiated the material necessities required to provide for the daily lives of the sisters. Commenting on the convent given over to the Sisters of Mercy at Limerick, Catherine found her style in furnishings had been secured. She wrote to Frances Warde:

> This house is fully in the old conventual style. Very bad all around as to neighborhood, but when within the gates quite a nice place, enclosed by the ruins of an abbey and green in every view. It has been put into the best repair and furnished in our own style.[38]

When Catherine assessed the merits of the convent first available in Birr, she reported that she found it better than adequate. Invariably she thought of material assets in terms of the good these assets could accomplish.

> This is a good old House, delightfully situated, fields or gardens all around it... As close to the

main street of the town as Baggot St. is to little James St., yet quite remote from all other buildings. Walls or hedges in every direction. It must be particularly healthy. Ten or twelve Sisters could be very well accommodated. There is one fine room, nearly as large as our first school room (now Community Room).[39]

With a talent for governance, for ordering, organizing, enabling, so that others found in themselves unsuspected capabilities, Catherine observed the beginning of a new foundation to create fresh energies and to promote new levels of bondedness and apostolic generosity. New challenges stretched many who had previously lain back, putting forth no more than ordinary effort. Spontaneously cheering on foundation makers, she exclaimed:

Hurrah for foundations, makes the old young and the young merry.[40]

Sharing her vision with those drawn to the same ideal, in a leadership that was more a dynamic of their life together than an authoritarian stance as foundress, Catherine succeeded in creating a sense of common endeavor where each one discovered a sense of being significant and purposeful.

A postulant whom she had brought to Birr outperformed all expectation.

Our postulant here is quite a different person from what she was in Baggot Street, useful in every way, nothing like foundations for arousing us all.[41]

Foundations provided opportunity to utilize talents. Needs everywhere were so great that they challenged the limits of ability to respond. Members felt how necessary was their complete participation and how much truly depended on their efforts. Members realized, too, the value of others' support and companionship. Experiencing such sharing, they developed qualities of belonging, acceptance, and mutual inspiration in every foundation that sprouted from Baggot Street.

Marveling at the change in Sister Aloysius Scott—the newly appointed superior handling her role in Birr—and astonished at her competence, Catherine proclaimed her, "the most vigilant, clever manager I have met in some time." Continuing her letter, she bemoaned:

> We put our candles under a bushel. She is in excellent health, has departed from her Carlow rules. Was up at 5 o'c and out visiting in the snow, when she would have been in bed in Baggot St. as was usually so.[42]

The story of Aloysius' untiring zeal in improving the convent building at Birr and in carrying out the evangelizing mission entrusted to them amazed the community back at Baggot Street who remembered a sickly companion who often took to her bed. When they heard of the hardships endured both from persons grown cold to their religion and from the cold itself, they understood better Catherine's cheer from Birr.

In her conviction of the importance of a good beginning, Catherine looked first toward the experienced women she had available, those first companions who could assume responsibility as superiors of new foundations. Having established four foundations within a fifteenth-month period, she would write:

> We are very near a stop—I should say a full stop. Feet and hands are numerous enough, but the heads are nearly gone.[43]

To develop, support, and enable the new superior to assume the responsibility of this role, Catherine's customary procedure in establishing a new foundation was to stay for the length of the Thirty Days' Prayer, in faith-filled trust that each would then carry out the new responsibility capably. After that, she entrusted the foundation community to begin to shape its own destiny.

Limerick proved to be a situation which required her presence past the established time limit. When faced with the public aspect of the role, to Catherine's surprise, Elizabeth Moore had become fearful and frightened.

I cannot go for a full month. No person of less experience could manage at present, and I am very insufficient for the task. As to Sister Elizabeth, with all her readiness to undertake it, we never sent forward such a fainthearted soldier, now that she is in the field. She will do all interior and exterior work, but to meet on business, confer with the Bishop, conclude with a sister, you might as well send the child that opens the door.[44]

Despite Elizabeth's unexpected timidity, Catherine reported her confidence and trust in the new superior's ability to assume the role once the initial anxieties dissipated.

I am sure this will surprise you. She gets white as death, and her eyes like fever. She is greatly liked, and when the alarms are a little over, and a few in the House, I expect all will go on well.[45]

Although Catherine could be frank in her explanation to her confidant, Frances Warde, as to why she could not leave Limerick, she was more circumspect in a letter to those at Baggot Street in providing the rationale for her own extended absence.

You must be aware that great caution is necessary selecting persons to commence an institution, where there is so much to fear and to hope. If a prudent, cautious beginning is made, there is every prospect of success. More judgment than I possess might be useful, but less would not distinguish between the characters that present themselves as to steadiness of purpose, capacity for the Institute, etc., etc.[46]

Having left Cork before her usual month stay had ended, Catherine planned an immediate return after the death of her niece Catherine. Writing to Frances Warde, Catherine explained that she had missed news of a mail packet boat leaving Dublin for Cork. She had intended to be on the first one available.

I have left her [Clare Moore] in an unfinished
state. She writes full of fears and doubts. Indeed
I know she has too much to encounter until the
way was made more easy for her. Please God I
will soon go there.[47]

Sister Clare Moore at twenty-seven was very young to
be left to deal with a very meticulous albeit devoted
bishop. Bishop Murphy very much admired his young
mother superior, thought highly of Catherine McAuley
and her institute, and made himself a father protector
none could excel. With her experience, Catherine hoped
to be able to assist in establishing the foundation in order
to alleviate heavy burdens on the new and inexperienced
superior.

Then too, Catherine felt responsible to enable one she
had entrusted with a leadership role. She had expected to
assist her longer but had been summoned away by the
critical illness of her niece. Left "in an unfinished state,"
Clare had written "full of fears and doubts," and
Catherine took the responsibility for her uneasiness. "Indeed I know she has too much to encounter until the way
was made easy for her."

Catherine admitted to Frances both her emotional
and physical trial, "I have suffered more than usual with
my old pain of sorrow and anxiety. My stomach has been
very ill."[48] But her priority, nevertheless, was to make the
way "more easy" for Clare Moore. She dealt with the reality that existed. If a sister were still fearful and full of
doubts, she needed to be strengthened, supported, and
educated for the task. With no time to indulge in healing
her own physical and emotional pain, Catherine concen-
trated on the difficulties and anxieties to be faced at Cork.

Without ever having heard the terms, Catherine understood the principles of both collegiality and
subsidiarity, and their essence was her practice. Faithfully presenting the traditional spirituality of the vowed
life, she nevertheless foreshadowed contemporary understanding of religious obedience in seeking advice of the
community and in sharing information and decision-
making with them. Her specification that "we have not
fully determined who will go" to help establish the Limerick foundation indicates the consultation involved in

choosing personnel for new foundations. Recording the management of personnel resources, Catherine noted

> For Booterstown we have marked out M. Cecilia, Superior—Ursula, J. Sausse, Lucy, Teresa. Sr. Scott will manage the collection business and the servants. [employment agency at House of Mercy][49]

Analysis of Catherine's letters reveals that she never uses an editorial "we." When she meant herself, she said "I" with self-confidence, candor, and humility.

Memoirs record that community business was discussed freely at recreation by all, creating a climate in which there was pride in contribution to shared goals. Sometimes this informal collegiality provided a source for whimsical banter at the evening recreation. That Catherine enjoyed the exchange is evident in her focusing on these scenes in letters in which she kept those away from Baggot Street informed about plans for new foundations. Undecided on a superior for Birmingham, Catherine notes that a young English postulant

> ...think she will be best suited for superior-ess... makes up most amusing reasons... affects to think all is now confirmed.[50]

That this was not an isolated instance of the humor they enjoyed together while endeavoring to decide on who would establish the next foundation is clear in Catherine's comment on another occasion:

> We announced that whoever could take tea without milk should go [to Birr] as Superior it being very difficult to procure it. Mother de Pazzi commenced this morning and has declared herself for an efficient candidate.[51]

Reporting the involvement of those at Baggot Street in the decisions affecting the institute, Catherine also sought the opinion of the sisters to whom she wrote. Concerned about whom to make superior in Birr, she requested Frances Warde's advice after explaining her own considerations. All of the women to whom she wrote as confidants were much younger than Catherine, but having placed them in positions of authority and responsibility, she treated them as peers. No letter of hers breathed even a word of condescension.

> At present I cannot fix my mind on any as head, but little Sister White, a perfect mistress, very faithful to her vocation and well-versed in all our ways. Tell me what you think of her for such a purpose. I fear a little tendency to party spirit, which yet remains, would be a great impediment.[52]

Whether prompted by a suggestion of Frances Warde or by her own indecision, Sister Teresa White was not chosen as superior, but rather Sister Aloysius Scott.

The practice of involving the sisters in decisions proper to them, which Catherine carried out constantly showed itself in matters small and great. At Birr, they found themselves in a house which had not been named. Everyone in the young community was involved in selecting the name. Catherine's description to Sister Cecilia Marmion sets the scene:

> The place where our convent stands has no particular denomination. We have proposed calling it Baggot Street. The little nonsensical proposition produced such immoderate laughing that I really was alarmed for Sr. Aloysius. I never saw her laugh in such a manner and I was choking. However, Baggot Street it is.[53]

Ecclesiastical Superiors and Dowries

Since nothing in Catherine required her to solve all difficulties without the help of others, her behavior freed all her superiors to call on similar resources. When Frances Warde sought Catherine's counsel in trying to place a sister in a convent other than Carlow, Catherine's correspondence reveals the supervisory role she played throughout the various foundations. It also highlights the practice of the time by which priest superiors, appointed by the bishop of the diocese, exercised authority over the local congregation of sisters.[54]

Dr. Fitzgerald, president of Carlow College, objected to receiving Miss Maher there because there were already several members of the family in that community, an imbalance that could create a family control of internal affairs. It was also a family that could not provide adequate dowry.

Catherine's letter indicates the approval necessary, and the controlling influence similarly exerted by Mr. Croke, pastor at Charleville and Mr. Daly, pastor at Galway.

> I rejoice in seeing a good Sister added to our order anywhere, but I would think it imprudent to press what Mr. Croke is opposed to. He never took such interest as he does now, and it is most fortunate and a great blessing indeed that he has taken the part of a guardian in full authority. All will go on well now, please God.
>
> I forget the little Sister. If her manners are not too plain, if she is rather nice than otherwise, and able to visit the poor, etc., etc., I think they would take her in Galway, provided what is promised would be secured. Mr. Daly requires that. If she is plain or speaks badly, she would not be acceptable to him.[55]

Part of the admission policy that the priest superiors took pride in and enforced wherever they were involved included that the candidate have an attractive manner in presenting herself to others. To be known as a "lady," within the connotations of nineteenth century society, was a decided asset. In addition to gifts of person, the candidate needed secure financial arrangements and an unblemished reputation. If she spoke ungrammatically or with a pronounced Irish brogue, or had worked for a living at any time, it was also a distinct impediment.

To help Frances understand Father Daly's careful scrutiny, Catherine likened him to the pastor in Carlow.

> He is to the Sisters a second Father Maher, and most particular. He would not take a Co. Galway person on such terms, but from a quarter where it will not be known I think I can induce him to take her... Mr. D is with them some time of every

day. He objected to a very nice young person to whom an uncle had left £300 because previous to that, she was for a few months only, at a most respectable dress and millinery warehouse in Clare St. He said the Co. Galway people would find out anything, and that it would be a certain injury.[56]

Catherine's practical common sense recognized the difficulty of accepting candidates with insufficient dowry, particularly in an area where there were no benefactors of wealth who might assist. Although she found the Galway Catholics quite ardent and believed that sound vocations could be added to their numbers if the dowry were not so necessary, she acknowledged there could be no support for the poor without the required dowries.

This is quite a pious Catholic place. I am sure there would be fifteen in the Convent before six months, if two or three hundred pounds could be taken, but the poor funds will not admit of it.[57]

Because Catholic wealth did not exist in such abundance that a foundation could presume on local alms to support works of mercy, dowries of sizable amounts (£600) were required from those who entered during Catherine's lifetime. Knowing from experience the needs of the poor and the wealth of the rich, she insisted that those who came from financially secure families pledge some share of their inheritance to support the works undertaken by the foundation. The major immediate source of revenue, the dowry was intended to provide more than lifetime security for its contributor within a stable group. Dowries also created the "poor fund," the money necessary to accomplish the works of mercy.

Commenting on those who had presented themselves for admission, Catherine explained:

We have four postulants... Three have nearly enough. One, Miss Bourke, who is fully arrived at the eleventh hour, has forty-seven pounds per annum during life and five hundred to bequeath.[58]

Catherine's astute judgment is evident in her recognition that there was not much actual wealth in Galway. It necessitated that she be very much on her guard to provide the foundation with a secure base.

Our order is greatly liked but there is really no money amongst the people, all high consequence and poverty.[59]

A few months later, Catherine wrote to Galway, urging Miss Maher's admission;

Sister Mary Frances... recommends her so strongly. I would advise you to take her if Father Daly has no objection. Her brother says he will give £15 per year for 10 years and defray every expense up to profession. In your letter on the subject, say that the first year should be paid in advance, and some security given for the remainder. I suppose her brother's note would be enough. Make out a full list of all she should bring, remember 4 cloaks, desk and work box, it may not be so easy to get a supply after she gets here, etc., etc.,[60]

While revealing the customary equipment which candidates brought with them, the essential policy that emerges was that of safeguarding a sister's private family background.

All these circumstances will be preserved in silence—you will never let the temporal wants of a Sister be known beyond its proper limits.[61]

Catherine herself often reduced the required dowry, although some ecclesiastical superiors kept tight control of that permission. Determined to fill his convent with proper ladies, that is, those with at least the £600 dowry, Bishop John Murphy's practice was to control admissions at Cork personally. Indignant with Catherine for admitting in his absence an excellent candidate with £300 plus yearly income for life, he characterized Catherine with clearly intended irony the "Sister of Divine Providence."

Subsequent to the misunderstanding which occasioned this sobriquet, Catherine noted:

> It will not be very easy to enter here. The terms are high, and no *abatement*... Every applicant is to be referred to the Bishop, provided [the superior] approves of them, and all settled by him.[62]

Written record of the financial arrangements usual for one entering the Sisters of Mercy is found in a letter Catherine wrote stating the amount of the dowry and the cost of the novitiate. The cost of one year's board and keep established at £25 highlights the sizable amount of the dowry required at profession.

> The appointed term of our probation is two years and a half—six months consideration and two years novitiate. The annual pension twenty-five pounds, at profession six hundred pounds.[63]

Other letters suggest that the dowry was less an absolute requirement than it sounded. Circumstances, both of personal gifts and foundation needs, altered the fixed nature of the requirement. But, since Catherine enforced a strict policy of the right to privacy about personal and financial matters, no records exist to indicate who paid the full amount and who did not.

In February of 1841, the saga of trying to obtain a place in another Mercy convent for Anna Maria Maher still continued. Birr, Catherine's last foundation in Ireland, was no exception in its financial requirements. Benefactors were few and could not be depended on to raise necessary funds; potential candidates had to be able to support themselves and their works.

> Poor Miss Maher, no chance here. Money, money is the theme. I entreated in favor of a candidate with £16 per year and £100 in hand, it was regarded quite insufficient. A convent never succeeded in this diocese, it is supposed from imprudent arrangements, the Bishop has given strict charges to the Vicar who is Superior.[64]

Acceptable candidates whom the sisters would have found a way to admit were often rejected in Cork, Galway, and Tullamore when they could not produce the £600 dowry required. Bishops had seen the failure of convents and the consequent plight of members forced to seek refuge with families.

This necessity for each foundation to have a way to finance itself on a regular basis made imperative Catherine's objective evaluation of the possibility of support existing in towns inviting Sisters of Mercy to live and work among their people. Her own resources had supported the beginnings at Baggot Street, but after five or six years, she knew how difficult it was just to finance operating expenses.

However, Catherine, with her generous heart and love for religious life, could not witness impoverished people and not make some effort to relieve them.

> I congratulate you on your happy increase, which you and I love so much that we will never frighten a candidate away for not having a bag of money. We will sooner give half our share than not multiply. The Lord and Master of our House and Home is a faithful Provider. Let us never desire more than enough—He will give that and a blessing.[65]

Fear for the institute itself was consequent upon overzealous financial watchfulness of ecclesiastical superiors. Catherine expressed anxiety whenever too much emphasis was put on financial security. Confiding a specific concern about Cork to Frances early in 1839 she mentioned hearing

> ...from Sister Mary Clare...whose account is not cheering. She feels very much their progress being kept back. Says that none like to propose, now there is so much scrutiny into family concerns and so much about means, though she add "we find that very limited means will suffice" and have plenty of money to spare.[66]

Catherine could show her annoyance or vexation when irritated by awkward methods of handling affairs. Because of Bishop Murphy's close investigation of a candidate's family finances, few wished to endure the scrutiny involved. Clare Moore confided to Catherine that she did not understand his purchasing the house next door in order to enlarge the convent when he was so reluctant to accept candidates. Commenting to Frances, Catherine wrote:

> The house next to them has been purchased to enlarge their convent, and this seems to perplex her more. No wonder, it should.[67]

Asceticism of Fund-Raising

The establishment of the House of Mercy had depleted Catherine's inheritance to such a degree that annual income from the remainder was minimal. Consequently, from the beginning Catherine knew the anxiety that the response to the call of the poor echoing from all sides would fail despite her best efforts.

Encouraged by her friend, Dr. Armstrong, that "a good subscription... might be easily raised... in such a fashionable neighborhood,"[68] she sought contributions in letters which began "C. McAuley takes the liberty of soliciting, etc."[69] These efforts were rewarded, but not without Catherine's being reminded by some who, regarding her a parvenu, replied with such offensive messages as "N. knows nothing of such a person as C. McAuley and considers that C. McAuley has taken a very great liberty in addressing her."[70]

Flourishing works required financial support. The very scope of the need which the House of Mercy was meeting indicates the extent of the distress; for at the same time that the Sisters of Mercy were responding to the cholera epidemic plaguing Dublin in 1832, newspaper accounts testify that over two hundred children daily were receiving instruction in the school, about sixty young women were lodged and supported while being prepared for employment, and more than one hundred sick poor were visited, provided with sustenance, and supported during convalescence.

Catherine accepted as an on-going asceticism the necessity of raising funds to support these ministries. In addition to the letters of solicitation presented by children to the homes of wealthy neighbors, early sources of revenue included collections at Masses in the chapel, donations prompted by the practice of charity sermons, and proceeds from bazaars.

All of these efforts met with success for a time, but their ability to produce the necessary income was short-lived as Catherine would eventually note: "Charity Sermon bad, chapel closed, bazaar unpromising."[71]

Charity sermons and bazaars, part of the social life of Dublin in the late eighteenth and early nineteenth century, were a standard source of revenue for the city's charities.

Attracting distinguished patrons who contributed "articles of utility, taste, and elegance [for] the Mart of Mercy,"[72] among whom were their royal highnesses, the Duchess of Kent and the Princess Victoria, the early bazaars could realize as much as £300.

Possibly the very success of the bazaar in 1834 occasioned Dean Meyler to cut off a source of funds which had been available since the dedication of the Baggot Street chapel. An ardent supporter of the Sisters of Charity and a critic of the new Institute of Mercy "rising of itself," Dr. Walter Meyler had succeeded Dr. Blake as parish priest at St. Andrew's in 1833. After first withdrawing permission for a second Mass on Sunday, in 1834 he closed the chapel to the public completely.

In a letter to her lawyer, Catherine reveals the need that soon followed.

> We begin to feel the want of the interest due on the Bond. Have we any chance of getting it soon? We have so often cautioned all those who supply us not to give any Credit on our account—I doubt they would now if we were to ask them.[73]

Since daily living needs were supported by careful investment of dowries of the sisters, this simple direct letter got immediate results.

Under duress to provide for the works of the House of Mercy, Catherine undertook to persuade Father James Maher of Carlow to preach a charity sermon for them at Baggot Street. Sermons of well known and admired preachers would attract the public at large to contribute, since an inspiring speaker "produces remarkable effects on the feelings which extend even to the ends of the purse, where if anything can be found, it is sure to come forth."[74]

Often beggar for her charities, her inheritance long since gone, Catherine was suppliant to Father Maher without losing her dignity.

> You created some little hope in my mind relative to the charity sermon which is appointed for the 18th of next month. Will you have pity on us now and we will feel particularly grateful and pray most fervently for you. I will look out anxiously for a favorable answer, perhaps I may not be disappointed.[75]

Writing to him earlier that month, Catherine had explained in jest that employing diocesan law, she would not be able to pay him the usual stipend of one pound or guinea because he had not completed the "week's attendance." Because this priest usually drew a crowd of wealthy patrons on whom Catherine depended for donations, she took a playful approach to get him to come back.

> I am sorry you did not complete the full weeks' attendance which according to the regulations of this diocese would have entitled you to one pound or guinea, which ever you liked best. The statutes are now most rigorously observed and I really cannot say, without making enquiry, whether a broken week is payable.[76]

Her letter was really an appeal to get this "drawing-card" back to Baggot Street to finish the week where many, coming to hear him preach, would be moved to donate more generously than usual. Catherine acknowledged the speciousness of her argument in a telling observation that articulated her practical sense of stewardship.

> You will excuse me I am sure, for taking this little advantage for you know although I should be simple as a Dove, I must also be prudent as a Serpent; and since there is very little good can be accomplished or evil avoided without the aid of money, we must look after it in small as well as in great matters.

Assuring him she did not want to lose his support, she became serious, but gave one more persuasive nudge in the postscript.

Most sincerely thanking you for past services and earnestly wishing for a renewal and continuance of the same, I remain My dear Father Maher in real sincerity, Your ever grateful, Mary C. McAuley. P S. Don't forfeit all chance of the pound — perhaps we can make up the week without violating the Law.

Catherine's deep sense of stewardship was an important facet of her spirituality. She employed it to rouse her own exertions, to call others to greater effort, as well as to negotiate to the advantage of any works of mercy.

Realistic about fund-raising activities, her sharp business eye evaluated Baggot Street's bazaar of April 1838 as having ended its usefulness as a source of revenue, especially as it no longer drew support from wealthy Protestants of Dublin. To Frances Warde she wrote

The Bazaar, all summed up after expenses, we will have about forty-five pounds, very unlike past days....I am told there were not ten Protestants in the room....I suppose we are done with Bazaars.[77]

Recognizing the diminishing effectiveness of the bazaar as a means of raising funds, the uncertainty of depending on daily solicitations for support, and experiencing the loss of daily collections in the chapel, Catherine determined to build a public laundry adjoining the House of Mercy which, in soliciting washing from fashionable households of the neighborhood, would both generate income and provide training to unskilled young women. From her investigations, a laundry seemed the best way to allay anxiety over money.

I did hope our Laundry would have been commenced by this, but no—delays innumerable. ...You would be surprised to know all that can be earned by this means.[78]

Catherine had assessed the outlook for the laundry as good, and communicated with a certain pathos her impatience or reluctance at having to let go some work that would have earned them an income.

New persons coming into the neighborhood every day. We are asked to take washing since the Townsend St. Asylum was removed to Donny Brooke [sic]. We have constant application. Yesterday, it went to my heart to send away a large parcel which would have paid well. In one Institution they earned 7 hundred pounds in 4 months, clear of all expenses.[79]

Appreciative of the aid of Fr. O'Hanlon, Catherine, nevertheless, gave primacy to God's blessing in a benefaction he obtained for them.

We are likely to have the long desired public Laundry built this season; through the Providence of God and the kindness of Mr. O'Hanlon we have got a Legacy nearly equal to the expense. What a comfort if I am permitted to see some secure means of supporting our poor women and children established, not to be entirely depending on daily collections which are difficult to keep up. We would soon have a valuable Laundry as the neighborhood is so good."[80]

Before the laundry would serve its purpose, Catherine was to learn a hard lesson from experience. A letter to her lawyer reveals a request that he send her the contract so that she might examine its wording. The contractor had provided her with only "a Room capable of being made into a Laundry."[81]

She found the contract "an unkind, unjust transaction," and no doubt communicated her displeasure effectively, since the contractor found her "graciously offensive."[82]

Kingstown Controversy

Ill-health plagued Baggot Street, traceable at least in part to overwork and poor diet. Having been urged by physicians she consulted to remove weakened sisters for a "change of air," preferably near the sea, Catherine purchased a property in Kingstown through the generosity of Sister de Chantal McCann, a young widow who had entered the community.

Although the intention was that only the work of visiting the sick poor would be undertaken at the "rest house," the sight of young girls loitering along the roads soon raised the question of establishing a school.

Proselytizers were active, there were no national schools, Baggot Street had sufficient members to provide some healthy sisters, and an enthusiastic curate argued the "spiritual destitution and moral degradation of these [young women] who though living within a few miles of the refined capital were [living] as though they were beyond the pale of Christianity and civilization."[83]

Without any available resources, Catherine offered the coach-house and stables for the purpose if fund could be obtained to convert them to schoolrooms. The parish priest, Fr. Bartholomew Sheridan, on being appointed pastor, had immediately built a church and already burdened with debt, offered only patronage. His zealous curate, nevertheless, considering that "a subscription for the purpose could not possibly fail though it would not do to open it just then,"[84] encouraged Catherine's confidence in Fr. Sheridan's vague promise to "do something."

With the assurance of long-term credit from a builder whom Fr. Sheridan brought to meet her, the work was undertaken with the only commitment, Catherine's promise to hand over the proceeds of that year's bazaar in order "to encourage a beginning."

The absence of any written agreement concerning the debt provides some extenuating excuse for the misunderstanding which ensued. Fr. Sheridan considered the responsibility was Catherine's; and she assumed it was his as parish priest.

To her lawyer, Mr. Cavanaugh, she set out the case with clarity and candor. It was impossible for her to have property in Kingstown that would not in some way serve the poor. Explaining that she had proposed giving the coach house, stable, and part of the garden with some gates, doors, and other materials for that purpose,

Catherine presented her dealings with the pastor and the builder and outlined for Mr. Cavanaugh the terms under which she had made a payment.

> Mr. Sheridan seemed quite disposed to promote it, and brought Mr. Nugent of Kingstown to speak about the plan. When that was fixed on, I most distinctly said, in the presence of Mr. Sheridan, that we had no means to give towards the expense, but to encourage a beginning, I promised to give all the little valuable things we had for a bazaar that year, and to hand over whatever it produced. We got 50 pounds, which I gave immediately to Mr. Nugent...
>
> While the building was going on, Mr. Nugent repeatedly said he had not any doubt of Mr. Sheridan's getting from the Board of Education a grant nearly sufficient to pay for it, and always added, "I will only charge what it costs me."
>
> Mr. Sheridan also said this with full confidence, and whenever I spoke to him of making application to the Board, he answered, "I am waiting for the account."[85]

When the bill was presented, however, Fr. Sheridan directed it to Baggot Street. This was a shattering experience for Catherine who firmly believed that a word pledged was a sacred honor. What she experienced differed much from what she had expected. She also evaluated the bill as inflated and the workmanship very ordinary.

> The letter which I enclose to you, Sir, says the account was furnished to me. It never was, nor could Mr. Nugent have ever, in sincerity regarded me as answerable to him. The charge seems to be a most extraordinary one for the coarse, plain work that is done.

In spite of the justice of her claim, she became legally responsible for the whole debt of "four-hundred and forty pounds" because the bazaar money had been registered as a payment on the bill and later had to sell part of the Kingstown property to complete payment. Catherine's zeal as well as her innate optimism in this case militated against her good business sense.

With a reputation as a "shrewd and close financier,"[86] Fr. Sheridan perhaps saw an opportunity to have the Baggot Street heiress donate property for the school, while allowing her to assume that the Board of Education would provide a grant to pay for it.

Near the end of her life, Catherine would still find it necessary to contradict a common misconception about the resources available at Baggot Street. Her ability to stretch monies through the industry and exertion of the sisters and the charity of friends allowed observers to assume that her inheritance was endless. She knew that the mother foundation was in no position to finance other houses, and nudged Mary Anne Doyle, gently but explicitly, to make that fact known to her bishop.

> I am going to propose myself as Deputy to Dr. O'Rafferty in the guardianship of your convent. Your good Bishop was much mistaken as to property here. We have ever confided largely in Divine Providence and shall continue to do so."[87]

Evaluator, Unifier, Communicator

Although the role of superior general would have been available to Catherine McAuley, her gift was to shape a familial community whose sense of unity transcended whatever formal governmental arrangements were necessary for the carrying out of their mission. Authority for her was service, enabling service. As the number of foundations grew, she was the evaluator, the unifier, and the communicator. She assessed what was happening, held them to their purpose, and connected the members of the Institute of Mercy to each other through her letters. She was also the animator, the term she regularly used to describe the primary role of one in a leadership position.

In addition to the bonds forged by their common mission and by her *Foundation Circulars,* Catherine's concern for each foundation, welcoming new members everywhere, urging "change of air" for those needing rest, rejoicing in the "affectionate interest ... [which brought them] one hundred miles to encourage and aid one another"[88] generated a centralizing influence, a sense of membership in one Institute of Mercy.

At the same time, insisting she was not a mistress general, she established each foundation as an independent convent, maximizing the responsibility and creativity of every member. While offering information and advice, her stance of non-interference in the affairs of a foundation as well as her empowering confidence in those entrusted with its progress emerges in her encouragement:

> Look at it with all your brains and you will soon make a great improvement.[89]

Catherine entrusted each of her leaders with positions of autonomy as superiors of independent foundations, yet the sense of relatedness is paramount. Alerting Teresa White by use of inhouse humor with ambiguous comments on the demanding Father Daly, the priest who dominated every aspect of the Galway foundation, she wrote:

> I cannot make up any excuse to write to Father Daly, as you say he is as kind as ever. If you would only complain, I could then alarm him by saying I would go to Galway immediately to look after my poor fatherless children.[90]

While Catherine regularly used the appellation, "children" and "grandchildren" to express her affectionate familial regard for members, she rarely took an authoritative stance with any foundation. What she succeeded in engendering was inter-involvement in an affectionate and loving community of adults who took pride in each other's accomplishments and who cared about each other's sufferings or difficulties.

In her leadership of the community, Catherine McAuley's governance might be viewed as significantly feminine in her emphasis on relatedness, awareness, and sensitivity to each individual. The "tender concern and regard" she held out in her original Rule as the desired mode of relationship among the Sisters of Mercy, her complete omission of any reference to the section in the Presentation Rule on "Titles," along with her intention that there be no class distinctions among the members of the community typify the familial spirit she endeavored to engender.[91]

Congratulations followed the announcement of new members in any of the foundations. Catherine, registering her annoyance with both Tullamore and Cork when she learned from visiting priests of the new members in each place, described Mary Anne Doyle as "doing the humble" in a tone that clearly revealed her disapproval that news of such blessings had not been shared.[92]

In contrast, Elizabeth Moore kept her informed about Limerick, allowing her to radiate her happiness.

> Your letter to London afforded me great happiness. God is evidently pleased with Limerick House. Five ceremonies in 14 months — this far outsteps all.[93]

Catherine enjoyed welcoming candidates from different places and backgrounds. Her letter to Frances rang happily about a new Scot who had joined the English and Irish postulants.

> I am quite renovated by a delightful addition to the flock. On Wednesday last, the first Scotch Sister that has joined an Irish community . . . The variety of accent is now quite amusing at recreation. She never was out of Scotland before.[94]

Priests visiting Baggot Street boasted of their special interest, often teasing Catherine that she was being outdone. Writing to Frances of a visit of Fr. Dan Nolan, a favorite of hers, she described a typical parlor happening which at the same time communicates the bond of relationship which existed.

> He told me you are still on the increase, quite outdoing old Mother House as to rapid progress.[95]

As members, one of another, in the Institute of Mercy, it was common practice for foundations to help each other get started. Catherine's remarks on models of collection records indicated that she herself organized administrative details in Birr.

Unity of community grew strong perhaps because it carried with it no easy familiarity nor presumptions. Catherine's letters reveal both her respect for her co-foundresses and her sense of herself as one among them. She seemed to feel no need to be first among equals. She waited genuinely even for those invitations that she somewhat inveigled. While it was not likely that any foundation would refuse her, she did await their permission to send a sick sister to them from Baggot Street, an action that proceeded as much from her view of herself and of them as from her innate courtesy to local pastors and local communities.

> A dear much valued Sister... would receive benefit from change of air... if you can admit her. I need not recommend her to your tenderness. I know she will experience every mark of affection... All expenses, of course, will be defrayed.[96]

Catherine's awareness that added expense would be a problem is amplified in a further observation that suggests the bishop in Tullamore assumed that Baggot Street was in a position to subsidize its daughter foundation.

> Your good Bishop was much mistaken as to property here. We have ever confided largely in Divine Providence and shall continue to do so.[97]

Prior to the establishment of Tullamore, correspondence with her lawyer reveals that Catherine was already experiencing a shortage of funds at Baggot Street. In an earlier letter to Mary Anne Doyle, Catherine had urged practical, enterprising effort to finance the work of the new foundation.

> I wish I could hear of your getting up a lottery or raffle occasionally....We have just had one.[98]

Her encouragement was not a directive; the decision was Mary Anne's. There is no record that Catherine ever transgressed the authority of the superior of an independent house.

Discouraging any inclination to dependency on Baggot Street, Catherine, nevertheless, modeled a spirit of union among all members of the institute, assuring Mary Anne:

> Let me know when you are closely pressed and I will divide with you be it ever so little.[99]

The "change of air" commonly prescribed by the medical profession of the age occasioned an instruction that encapsulates the affection, solicitude, and practical nursing awareness characteristic of Catherine.

> Will you, my Dear, get the room ... prepared for her ... and give her all the care you can for a little time? ... A little broiled meat, or whatever she tells you she can take, not to get up till breakfast time except for Mass and that [when] she feels able. Not to go out except she likes to try a short walk. *Great tenderness in all things.*[100]

Catherine tried to insure that the sick would not be taxed beyond their strength. In another letter in which she writes to animate and cheer a sister away recuperating, and sensitive that awareness of activity at Baggot Street eased feelings of separation, Catherine noted that the community devotions included the Thirty Days Prayer for the success of the establishment of the Birmingham foundation.

> We commenced the 30 Days prayer on Thursday in place of the Psalter. The substance of petition: that God will graciously direct all the arrangements to be made for the establishment of the Convent in Birmingham. As I gave previous notice and entreated the pious cooperation of all, I am sure we have it. I do not wish you to say the long prayer, but think of the intention at Mass when you can.[101]

So much of Catherine's style of tenderness to the sick and of her manner of governance can be found encapsulated in this excerpt. She did not give peremptory orders.

She sought for active participation by advance notice, by requesting her community support her in her need for guidance and direction by joining in prayer. Yet she made sure those weakened by illness did not feel responsible for an added duty.

Priest visitors also brought news that was not so welcome. In a formidable letter to Angela Dunne, superior at Charleville, Catherine, sensing danger to the institute and its mission, demonstrated her leadership. In a letter direct, clear, and to the point, she spoke forcefully to correct what to her was a serious issue for the institute— the possibility of the foundation's breaking up.

> My dear Sister M.Angela, the Charleville foundation has been a source of great anxiety to me. One of the curates called on me in Cork asking in a kind of disguised way, but like as if called on to do so, would any of the Sisters be sent to Limerick—would Sister Delaney?[102]

Arguing against removal of the sisters because of any hardship or deprivation they were enduring, Catherine then proceeded to declare her feelings about this turn of events.

> I felt quite disturbed, as if we were like persons in the world, changing our house or lodgings on trifling occasions. Since I left Cork, Mr. Reardon the Monk, made some such inquiry.[103]

Evaluating the situation, she reminded Angela that the local bishop was involved and that a unilateral decision should not be made. Her most cogent argument, however, was that she feared that they would experience the loss of God's blessing by retreating from a situation unless compelled by necessity.

> What could excuse us before God for casting off any charge which we had freely undertaken except compelled by necessity to do so? Are not the poor of Charleville as dear to Him as elsewhere And while one pound of Miss Clanchy's five hundred lasts, ought we not to persevere and confide in His Providence?[104]

Catherine's sense of stewardship was strong. Money given in a particular area was to be utilized for the poor of that area. Her own inheritance she had committed entirely to the poor of Dublin and vicinity. Each town where a foundation was established was expected to furnish necessary funding. It was inconceivable to Catherine that Sisters of Mercy leave before the money contributed for Charleville had been used to advantage there.

Her knowledge of the workings of Charleville suggest more of the role of mother general than of peer superior. When she sent Sister Angela Dunne to Charleville, Catherine had sent her yearly income along with her. Aware that the benefactor, Mrs. French, had pledged an annual gift, and knowledgeable about the rate of interest, Catherine insisted:

> I had a letter from Mrs. French. She says that fifty pounds per annum will be paid. Your 30 and the interest will make 97; surely that will do.[105]

Convinced that holding fast in conditions of struggle and personal suffering brought untold blessings to them and to the poor for whom they labored, Catherine reassured Angela calmly with one of her most quoted injunctions:

> Put your whole confidence in God. He never will let you want necessities for yourself or children. It would afflict me and would be a disgrace to our order to have a breakup.[106]

This call of the mother superior for generous response and self-forgetfulness was in the best traditions of religious dedication. It is also an example of the major office of true leadership, to release unsuspected strengths and untested potentials. It was not Catherine's style to become cold, angry, or stiff in person or on paper. Her indignation, when it flared out in her letters was finely controlled and surrounded by affectionate salutations and conclusions. With a natural gift for leadership, Catherine exhorted and encouraged while inveighing against whatever situations or conditions needed correction, inspiring trust, heroic efforts and greater generosity in others.

It is clear that the crisis in Charleville continued, since Catherine wrote eight months later after providentially visiting the foundation:

> There was danger of all breaking up, and my heart felt sorrowful when I thought of the poor being deprived of the comfort which God seemed to intend for them. I made every effort and praised be God, all came round. The first stone of a nice convent was laid on our dear Festival, the 24th, and leaving all in joy and happiness we proceeded to our present abode on the same favored Day."[107]

What a boon it would be to have a record of her "every effort." The letter suggests how contagious was her own ardent enthusiasm for Christ and his poor and how it rekindled zeal, hope, courage, and cheerful service in younger sisters.

Chapter X

MISSION AND MINISTRY

An observant, practical woman, Catherine McAuley looked and saw what transpired around her in early nineteenth century Ireland. She listened and heard what reflected the joy and pain of life. Reflecting on what she experienced, she learned ways to be helpful to body, mind, and spirit. She absorbed the existing reality of poverty, sickness, and ignorance while struggling to develop better resources to alleviate these ills.

The pressure of population growth on the means of subsistence,[108] coupled with the difficulties inherent in Ireland's proximity to and constitutional association with England through the Act of Union, created a culture of poverty for the majority of the Irish people. The rural poor found themselves in desperate competition for minute land holdings, while in the cities unemployment was accompanied by overcrowded housing, poverty, and dirt.

Years of quiet study of the Gospels had given Catherine McAuley an intuitive theology of mission which flowed essentially from her keen penetration of the mystery of the poor, and found expression in a prayer in her own handwriting: "My God, look down with pity and mercy on your afflicted poor and grant us grace to do all that we can for their relief and comfort."[109] She had acquired in the twenty years of her "hidden life" with the Callaghans a firm conviction that it is in dealing with poverty in whatever form it takes that one communicates the gospel message that God is present in this world. Because of this conviction, diversity in ministry was common from the inception of the House of Mercy.

Catherine, whose life had given her entree to both the affluent and the impoverished, had penetrated the assumptions that led to misunderstanding in both groups, closed and isolated from each other. Her compassionate nature reached out wholeheartedly and primarily to the poor in their wretchedness; but she understood that the layer upon layer of ignorance, misfortune, bigotry, and hatred which restrict human liberty entrap both rich and poor.

Today's theological language of mission speaks in terms of human liberation—liberation from sickness, disease, and ignorance—of evangelization, and of pastoral care. Catherine's scope was equally wide and encompassed similarly diverse activities.

New foundations grew from Catherine's gospel vision of the response that the Institute of Mercy could make to the needs in Ireland and England. There was so much to be done with so few resources that she did not want any foundation groups to settle down to complacent or comfortable service when so many suffering people were calling out for relief. Her policy, "When you have enough, divide." was a constant clarion call. She congratulated those who did divide and urged on those who were slow to progress.

> It gives me great consolation and relief to find
> Carlow so prepared to divide. I think they will
> now keep it up. Liverpool is expected to be next.
> In about another year Limerick will be starting
> and Cork could step out but Doctor Murphy will
> be slow and sure.[110]

At one time, Catherine had felt her presence necessary to new beginnings. Experienced in meeting needs without losing the shape, character, or original spirit of the work entrusted to her, she realized as the community grew that her sisters too shared her ideals, and had grown in their ability to extend the work of the institute. Holding every foundation as part of the total effort for God and the poor, she rejoiced in the precedent Carlow was setting.

To divide—to give away part of a foundation's strength and potential—in order to establish a convent to respond to particular needs in a new location, for Catherine meant that Sisters of Mercy had opportunities for a devoted, generous service which "settling in" militated against.

The magnitude of the need and her own zeal for the relief of the poor caused Catherine to bewail that the Naas convent belonged "to the clutch called creepy crawley," that there was "too much caution in Cork," and that Tullamore was a "creep mouse in such a cause"—the courage to respond to the needs of another area by a willingness to divide.[111] In contrast, her observation of the fervor and initiative of those zealously undertaking a new foundation despite diminished numbers cheered her into speculating that ". . . too many women living together engender troublesome humors of mind and body.[112]

Such an observation may have been motivated by her own advice to "Turn what you can into a jest," for even though willing, the parting with much needed experienced sisters brought forth the admission a few months later that Baggot Street was "reduced to infancy again."[113]

As she grew in the experience of making foundations, Catherine discerned those practices which augured for success of the new institute of "walking nuns." The importance of presenting the nature of the Sisters of Mercy to the inhabitants of a new town without delay, she knew was urgent and advised each foundation to "Commence the visitation as soon as possible. . . while we place all our confidence in God, we must act as if all depended on our exertion."[114]

To call attention to the nature and purpose of the new community, profession and reception ceremonies were scheduled promptly as public occasions, since "All possible excitement is required."[115] Ahead of her time in recognizing the value of a media event, Catherine knew that this created awareness among those who could give financial backing, those who could encourage others to join the congregation, and most importantly those who could learn to expect and welcome the services of the Sisters of Mercy.

Flexibility and Diversity

Whatever would foster the relief of the poor found a ready response in Catherine, creating a flexibility in her practices which no doubt was a factor influencing the spread of the institute. During the Limerick foundation, she observed that "The poor here are in the most miserable state. The whole surrounding neighborhood one scene of wretchedness and sorrow."[116] She knew that the need was so great that if she left before they held a public reception, admitting new members, it would be necessary for her traveling companion to remain to help since the poor would accept only the service of the "nuns." Willing to accommodate the prejudice of the people they had come to serve, who "are very sharp and say queer things... don't like the net caps [postulants] too well to speak to them, but turn to the others," Catherine declared that "Every place has its own particular ideas and feelings which must be yielded to when possible."[117]

Convinced of the action of God in her life and in the life of the institute, Catherine resisted only those accommodations that would change the nature of the Institute of Mercy. She felt it imperative to be faithful to the call she had received. Without fail, she remained open to whatever promoted the good works of the institute which in her vision could, with great flexibility, accommodate within its mission different persons, different life experiences, and the needs of different localities.

Shortly after the establishment of the convent in Tullamore, an inquiry from a parish priest requesting that Catherine indicate the qualities she looked for in a prospective Sister of Mercy prompted her to delineate what she thought as generally requisite. Giving priority to the desire to "be united to God, and serve the poor," she stipulated also that a candidate should have "a particular interest for the sick and dying." While elaborating on other desirable characteristics, Catherine emphasized her openness to anyone drawn to the life of a Sister of Mercy in noting "that this is what seems generally necessary. I am aware exceptions may be met."[118]

That this willingness to make exceptions extended also to financial arrangements is reflected in correspondence Catherine conducted with an English bishop who inquired about having a group of young women prepared to carry on the works of mercy in his diocese. While stating the standard policy, she makes clear it is not an absolute:

> The pension for each during the novitiate is twenty-five pounds per annum—if circumstances required a reduction it would be made.[119]

The time distribution subsequently sent for the bishop's information and approval carried the notation that while its divisions had been found "well-adapted to the duties of the Order," they also were "subject to any alteration that place or circumstances might require."[120]

Catherine's flexibility as a leader, clearly evident in substantive matters, could without hesitation accommodate accidentals. This allowed her quick reversal of advice to Frances Warde regarding the type of veil to be worn in Wexford. Although she had pleaded that Frances not "wear the cashmere. . . the cape is not nice," a week later she revoked her objection:

> There cannot be any objection to your wearing the cashmere cloaks if you prefer them. I believe the Sisters everywhere think they have a more religious appearance. It must be difficult to preserve them nice looking in winter. The frequent cleaning in Dublin would soon make them look very bad.[121]

An appearance that could not be derided was important to Catherine. She expected Sisters of Mercy to dress simply in order to identify with the poor, but a neat and presentable appearance was part of her sense of mission.

When Daniel O'Connell, with a rhetoric uniquely Irish, saluted the new community of "walking sisters," he called attention to feet neatly dressed as identifying the *lady* hidden under simple garb and quiet, gentle manners. Catherine recorded the gist of his comments for the entertainment of all:

> No country on the face of the earth is like Ireland. Look at the fairest portion of creation, educated and possessing all the virtues that adorn and endear life. Forsaking their homes, their families, and friends, entering a convent in the morning of their days to devote long lives to piety and the promotion of virtue. Look at the Sisters of Mercy (hear, hear), wrapped in their, long black cloaks, they are seen gliding along the streets, in this humble attire, while a slight glance at the foot shows the educated Lady. Thus they go forth, not for the purpose of amusement or delight. No,

they are hastening to the lone couch of some sick fellow creature, fast sinking into the grave with none to console, none to soothe. They come with hope and consolation, and bring down with their prayers the blessing of God on the dying sinner, on themselves, and on their country (cheers). O such a country is too good to continue in slavery. (Great cheering.)[122]

Catherine enjoyed the speech with the others, as each claimed for her foot the tribute of praise. She then used the opportunity to advertise homemade boots which the sisters in Baggot Street were wearing, continuing her letter with a full explanation:

They have lately made some very nice cloth boots, and got them soled and capped with leather. When finished they do not cost quite 4 shillings... They are exceedingly neat and warm—any kind of stocking will do. I have been long recommending the homemade boots, both for neatness and economy.[123]

Catherine's passion that those mutually drawn by a love of God to the service of others strive to model the gospel life, bestowing the gift of themselves with cheerful, generous, compassionate service, revealed itself over and over. Her focus on "boots" as reflective of desirable economy had also surfaced in an earlier bit of rhyme. Holding out the ideal in light verse, she both encouraged higher aspiration and honored the psychological reality of a young sister who would eventually lead the Sisters of Mercy to Newfoundland.

My dear Sister Muse, I am sorry to find
That sweet holy poverty's not to your mind
What in your case would a poor girl do,
But look for a cobbler to mend her old shoe.
Is soling and healing a language obscure,
To those who have freely made vows to be poor.
How many bleak winters were safely passed
    through
With nothing to keep out the wet but a shoe,
And now, when we should be abounding in fruit,

We are wishing to dress up our foot in a boot.
The advocates here did wisely discover,
That a break in a stocking, the boot would quite
    cover.
Oh! shame for a Sister of Mercy to own
That she'd cover up, what she ought to have
    sewn.
May we not fear 'tis the enemy lurking
On our fears and our fancies so artfully working
Who at the word cobbler would teach us to blush
And whisper, get boots made of leather and
    plush.
But where reason is not, all reasoning is lost
Then, pray get the boots to keep out the frost. [124]

If boots which "keep out the wet" furthered the visitation of the sick, an essential duty of a Sister of Mercy, Catherine's clear sense of mission countenanced their use.

Her correspondence with the bishop of Birmingham asserts not only the flexibility of the community life as lived by the Sisters of Mercy, but also the diversity of ministry which was already accommodated by their daily horarium. The "Daily Distribution of Time" reveals that some entered upon duties in the school, some to the visitation of the sick, and some to the instruction of adults.

Care of the Sick

The duty that was the special hallmark of the new congregation, the duty which caused them to be called in derision "the walking nuns," the duty which primarily challenged their being perceived as "proper" religious since they did not maintain enclosure, was visiting the sick. Not a social call, to visit the sick meant to render both spiritual and corporal works of mercy—comforting the sick, support for the dying, prayers, home nursing care, family counseling, housekeeping instructions, and tutoring in sound health procedures. Catherine was convinced that the purpose of nursing the sick was to restore them to health in as total a way as possible.

It is generally agreed that among her many gifts, Catherine McAuley's own special charism was the care of the sick. Her long years of nursing Mrs. Callaghan as well as her personal tutoring by family medical men and her experiences in caring for the sick poor in their homes and in hospitals gave her an educated ability to evaluate illness.

To Sister Cecilia Marmion, who had been sent to Birr for "change of air," Catherine wrote:

> I am sorry you wrote until you were fully rested. In about ten days I expect to hear of great improvement, please God.[125]

With practiced nurse's eye, Catherine could predict with some assurance how long recuperation would take and knew that unless Cecilia were exposed to some other contagion, she would improve in less than two weeks.

Catherine had learned much about the causes of disease, having lost most of her family and many of her friends and associates to fever, tuberculosis, and cholera, the disease that plagued the Irish. Prevention of disease therefore had a high priority with her. Whenever she heard of sickness in any foundation house, she immediately wrote to urge proper care:

> I have been very uneasy about you since I heard how you have been affected. Yet I know you are not sufficiently cautious, and this is what I fear most. Now let me entreat you not to be going through the new convent or out in the garden even the mildest day during this month without carefully wrapping up.[126]

Small details record the quality of care she extended to the sick as well as the expert skill with which she diagnosed those illnesses she observed or personally attended:

> She died on the tenth day of violent fever. She was exactly like a person in cholera, cold and purplecolored. Some kind of circulation was kept by wine, musk, cordials and warm applicants, but no hope of recovery from the first 3 days.[127]

Service rendered by Catherine and her young community when the deadly cholera epidemic struck Dublin only three months after the Institute of Mercy was established had given her a clear understanding of the treatment and progress of this disease. With the approval of the archbishop, Catherine had responded to the request of the board of health that she and her associates staff the improvised hospital at the Townsend Street Depot. Panic and fear of the hospitals, accompanied by consequent concealment of the disease, had made the plague an even graver threat. The presence of the Sisters of Mercy not only alleviated this situation, but at a time when nursing was not a recognized profession, so improved the quality of care of the patients that the death rate was one of the lowest on record.[128] This accomplishment was specifically attributed by the chief physician to Catherine's own administration.

Rotating the sisters in shifts of four hours, Catherine herself remained from early morning until late at night, supervising the care and consoling the dying. So extraordinary was the devotion of Mary Anne Doyle who spent so many hours on her knees moving from bed to bed that she suffered from severe swelling for long months afterward, that Catherine sang her praises in verse which testifies to the spirit that permeated even the most difficult days.

> Dear Sister Doyle, accept from me
> For your poor suffering martyrs
> A laurel wreath to crown each knee
> In place of former garters.
>
> Since fatal cholera appeared
> You've scarce been seen to stand,
> No danger for yourself e'er feared
> When death o'erspread the land.
>
> While on your knees from bed to bed
> You quickly moved about,
> It did not enter in your head
> That knees could e'er wear out
> You've hurt the marrow in the bone
> Imploring aid and pity,
> And every Cardinal in Rome
> Would say you saved the City.

Now that the story of your fame
In Annals may be seen,
We'll give each wounded knee a name—
Cholera and Cholerene!

Only a few lines in her letters reveal the respect in which the nursing skills of the Sisters of Mercy were held. But when Tullamore's expansion and new convent were underway, a passage to connect with a local hospital was included in the planning:

> They have commenced a convent in Tullamore. Mr. Malloy, a very wealthy, pious Catholic, has taken the house they are in for a hospital. Their convent is to be joining the new school, and they are to have a passage to the hospital through their present garden.[129]

Care of the sick at home and in hospitals, begun in 1827, remained a clear mission of the Sisters of Mercy in each foundation. That a wealthy doctor sought to associate his hospital with Sisters of Mercy resulted directly from their practice of daily nursing visitations to the sick.

Concern for Women

Catherine's conviction of the potential contribution of women to the betterment of society, an emphasis not reflected in the Rule she used as a model, affords insight into her vision by that very fact.

> The Sisters shall feel convinced that no work of charity can he more productive of good to society or more conducive to the happiness of the poor than the careful instruction of women.... Wherever a Religious woman presides, peace and good order are generally to be found.[130]

From the initial impetus to build a house which could provide both temporary refuge for women and opportunity for their employment, Catherine's concern for women would be reflected in the education afforded for both rich and poor.

An encounter with a young lad in Birr who shifted her trunks from coach to coach on one of her journeys increased her zeal to educate native Irish women who would in turn supervise the education and training of their children. Pouring out appreciation and concern in describing the "fine little boy who brought the great trunk [but] would not take any payment, 'Ah sure mam, I'll be ped at home,'"[131] Catherine voiced her distress over kind-hearted, bright children whose speech patterns insured they would fetch and carry their life away.

Educational Vision

Part of Catherine's native skill at governance led her to recognize immediately an opportunity to extend or expand works of education for the poor. Her quick and practical eye discovered the benefit of attaching poor schools to the national school board when she found one flourishing in Limerick. Among the bishops of Ireland there was strong disagreement about the wisdom of Church involvement in the national schools. Catherine, firmly convinced they presented no threat to faith, supported Dr. Murray's stance by taking steps to affiliate the Baggot Street school with the national board.

Encouraging all her houses to do the same, she buttressed her arguments with evidence that Mr. Carlile, a vehement anti-Catholic supporter of the apostate priest of Birr, had resigned from the national school board in fierce opposition to its policies. This assured her that the national board intended to protect the rights of Catholics.

> The unfortunate Crotty is indefatigable in his evil works. He is joined by Mr. Carlile, who was one of the Commissioners of Education. They have the same church and preach the same doctrine, that nothing is to be feared but popery! This speaks well for National Education. Had Mr. Carlile found it likely to injure the Catholic Church, he would not have abandoned it.[132]

However, word that Mary Anne Doyle was considering taking the training course to learn the examination system for the national schools occasioned a letter from Catherine, voicing her chagrin at the report. Catherine's spontaneous, "Surely not!" issued from her clearsighted view that Mary Anne's responsibility as superior directing all the works of the Tullamore foundation prohibited her devoting herself full time to such an all-absorbing activity.

Catherine's leadership style was such that she offered alternative possibilities, encouraging Mary Anne to proceed with the development of the monitress system of the national schools while honoring her role as the superior and the one responsible for the appropriate decision:

> Would it not be better to try to get a well-qualified Monitress from the Model School until your sisters know the Method? They sent us such a one from Limerick, quite a poor girl. . . . She should be paid a small salary out of what the Board allows. . . . There could not be a more delightful school than they have in Limerick. If one of your Sisters went there Sister Hartnett, who is exceedingly clever, would teach her in a very short time. . . . I need not add that you have this house at your command if you think of Dublin.[133]

With the gospel as her model, Catherine's moral authority in addressing her foundations conveyed not the slightest coercion or control, but rather communicated a nurturing concern. The scope of options the letter offered provides insight into Catherine's vision, showing as it does that she endorsed sisters obtaining appropriate education for the service to be rendered, encouraged the various foundations to serve as resources to one another, and supported incorporating qualified laity to help with the work. Of note is Catherine McAuley's genuine sensitivity regarding justice toward the poor in the letter's evidence that she was paying monitresses well before payment became official in 1845.[134]

The letter illustrates further the openness to new ideas, the readiness to adapt and assimilate, the ability to learn from the experience of contemporaries, and the desire to share that experience with others that fostered the rapid spread of the Institute of Mercy.

Her years of mature experience of the whole spectrum of human need encompassed by the corporal and spiritual works of mercy may have prompted Catherine McAuley, when compiling the Rule for the Sisters of Mercy, to omit that section of the Presentation Rule which stipulated that "this Religious Institute shall admit none into their schools but poor Children."[135] "Need" was Catherine's touchstone; ministry response followed accordingly.

Within two years of the establishment of the Carlow foundation, it became clear that, although there was a flourishing school for the poor conducted by the Presentation Sisters, no one ministered to the children of the new middle class. Children from these families were too well-off to be accepted in the poor schools and not of sufficient means to be admitted to the existing finishing schools for the rich.

Convinced that this group formed "the connecting link between the high and the low classes," Catherine sanctioned the pension school begun by Frances Warde as a work of "the utmost importance."[136]

The success of Carlow's pension school caused her to encourage others in Charleville, Tullamore, and Cork.

> The pension school in Carlow is making great progress. You must get their regulations. It is quite simple and does not seem to add to their toils. Some sweet young persons amongst them who bid fair become Sisters. They are all interested, and some prefer it to any other duty.
> ... They have already commenced [one] at Naas and have 18 pupils, and also a poor school.[137]

Catherine encouraged whatever ministry of mercy fell within the competence of the sisters and the needs of those around them. Her argument in support of the pension schools was cogent and succinct. The teaching system was simple and did not add unreasonable burdens; the pupils having more advanced educational and social backgrounds, the school was fertile soil for the growth of vocations; and the talents of some sisters made them prefer this assignment.

Contemporaries in improving the lot of the Irish poor such as the prominent temperance preacher, Rev. Theobald Matthew, found a staunch supporter in Catherine McAuley. Renowned throughout Ireland for bringing back sobriety, peace of mind, and practice of religious duty to thousands of men and women, Father Matthew was significantly involved in encouraging that Sisters of Mercy be established in Birr to restore the peace disturbed by a schism led by a former curate.

Writing to Frances Warde, Catherine reflected on the power of Father Matthew to do immense good through the grace of God. Her observation clearly reveals that she did not romanticize the poor she served so diligently. She did not blame or resent them for being the way they were, but neither did she try to cover their faults or pretend not to see them.

> ... what the special grace of God can produce tho' bestowed but on one man, yet so as to go forth amongst millions. Through the agency of his touch, creatures who never could keep a promise made to God or man, and who frequently violated the most solemn oath, when intemperance was in question, persons of strong mind and good education, never have given evidence of such resolution as these millions of weak, ignorant, obstinate creatures are now manifesting.[138]

The "weak, ignorant, obstinate creatures" were those for whom she labored and for whom she travelled hundreds of miles in carriages, on boats, and on foot to manifest God's compassionate love and mercy. She served them in their reality, put no expectations upon them out of her own need, and rejoiced when anyone could bring peace into their lives.

While Father Matthew was with great success devoted to overcoming the evil of drunkenness for which the Irish were excoriated by the Anglo-Irish and others worldwide, there were too few to pick up his slack, the need for education to develop the physical, intellectual, and spiritual potentialities of the Irish.If the temperance pledge and regular church-going were to lead to productive lives and not to quiet desperation and feigned accommodation to the miseries around them, leadership beyond the temperance pledge was needed.

Catherine understood that to live in sobriety, a sense of dignity and self worth are essential. Constant exposure to indignities, frustration, and abject poverty induces a pain of life difficult to bear. Forgetfulness or oblivion is sought as an escape. Houses and schools of Mercy provided job training and basic education for the poor that made possible a life of more personal independence.

Catherine, who may have thought of sobriety as the necessary first step to becoming industrious, provident, and peaceable, could not mention Father Matthew except in tones of greatest admiration: "What an agent he has been in the hands of God."[139] She honored his work as providing an impetus toward liberation of the human person and saw his effort as far surpassing her own.

Global Vision

A global vision which far exceeded the bounds of Ireland, and further expanded the diversity of ministries as needs of culture and environment dictated, was characteristic of Catherine McAuley. Learning that the priest appointed by Archbishop Murray to work in Nova Scotia was having great difficulty finding clergymen willing to accompany him, Catherine, devoid of any fear when the spread of the kingdom was the issue at hand, eagerly offered her services for the rough work to be encountered in a new region.[140] Not the least discouraged by the priest's protest that Nova Scotia was too primitive to allow success since "vocations must come from an advanced state of religion and education," Catherine countered with a conviction which her experience with public professions in new foundations had corroborated: "You have often seen a recruiting party come into a town or city. No one appeared anxious to become a soldier... the drum, and fife, and cockade, aroused new thoughts, new hopes, and new projects, and the recruiting party is soon followed by a new supply for the ranks. Make the experiment!"[141]

Although her offer was not accepted, another route to the Americas for the Institute of Mercy opened up when the bishop of Newfoundland sent a prospective candidate to Baggot Street to be prepared for this mission. By this time, Catherine's failing health prohibited her considering herself for this foundation, although she admits having expressed a "wish for St. Johns."[142]

Calling attention to the "rage for Missions" while recognizing the reality that Baggot Street had become in large part, a novitiate training ground, Catherine described the visit of the bishop of Charleston, South Carolina, come to plead for his diocese.

> Have you heard of the great rage for Missions? The Bishops of foreign districts going about to get all the religious sisters they can. Dr. England from Charleston celebrated Mass here this morning and gave a most animating exhortation in a loud voice. He said: 'Fear nothing, follow Paul in peril, pestilence, and famine that you may be his glorious associate for time and eternity. The moment you get into his path you will feel as if in Heaven.'[143]

If Baggot Street had had sisters to give, Catherine would have parted with them as generously as she had parted with those for other places in Ireland and England.

With no way to honor his request, yet unable to reject him flatly, Catherine let him experience the poverty of personnel at Baggot Street.

> After breakfast we assembled all the troops in the community room from all quarters— Laundry, Dining Hall, etc., etc. By chance 2 were in from Kingstown—we made a great muster.... His Lordship was obliged to acknowledge that we are poor dependents on the white veil and caps. We certainly look like a community that wanted time to come to maturity, reduced to infancy again as we are.[144]

Despite the clear drain it was to divest herself of experienced sisters, each call for service, no matter where, found ready response as long as there were any to give. No new work was ever seen as threat to those already begun.

Not every foundation of a Convent of Mercy was universally welcomed. Catherine's first convent outside Ireland was greeted by a London press giving scurrilous welcome to the "female agents of the Papacy," one intimating the convent in Bermondsey was a house of prostitution and another questioning the use of "lady" to describe any of those coming to inhabit it.[145]

Although the hostility of the London press created anxiety for some in Ireland who dearly loved the Sisters of Mercy, Catherine's equanimity was not disturbed.

> I am sure Mr. O'Hanlon is a little alarmed at the angry things which are said in the English papers—he gave me 10,000 cautions yesterday.[146]

Her sense of humor permitted her to approach without intimidation the country that was nemesis even to the Anglo-Irish who drew their style, manners, and traditions from England, accepting without question the assumption that England had superior customs, culture, and conventions in all areas of society. In a jesting reference to the formality of English manners, Catherine reported that on the journey to Bermondsey:

> We laughed and talked over the adventures of the night, particularly my traveling title, changed from your Kitty to friend Catherine, an improvement, you will say.[147]

In spite of negative newspaper accounts, the arrival of the Sisters of Mercy in London became a social event. Elizabeth Agnew's prestige as the author of the best seller, *Geraldine,* and the imminent reception ceremony for Lady Barbara Ayre, daughter of the Earl of Newburgh, the first member of English nobility in centuries to enter a religious congregation, soon resulted in long lists of titled guests calling at the convent to offer their patronage.

A long letter depicting the events of the foundation in Bermondsey recorded the surprises, joys, comedies, pomp and circumstance, works begun, longing for Dublin, but nothing of the cold and unwelcome arrival the foundation party experienced due to the illness of the priest who had been instrumental in bringing them to London.

Describing the reception, Catherine named all the titled personages who sat in the sanctuary. Not overawed by the splendid accoutrements worn by the presiding bishop, the presence of over four thousand illustrious guests, nor the feathered and diamonded novice Lady Barbara Ayre and her titled family, she lightheartedly lamented the exacting demand on her own energies in the repeated climbing of the nine steps that led to the bishop's throne in front of the high altar.

> Kitty had to go up and down 18 times, 3 times
> with each, indeed I might have said, Poor
> Kitty.[148]

A woman of less character might have preened a bit
over the conquest of English society; Catherine's letters
show that her sense of fun had full play. That these Irish-
born Sisters of Mercy were found to be women of culture
and refinement astonished those who called upon them.
Catherine richly enjoyed their amazement.

> They are also very kind and evidently astonished
> to find such wild Irish—nuns. Mrs. Agnew partic-
> ularly pleased with "the young lady Superior";
> acknowledges she did not expect her daughter
> would meet such a companion in the south of
> Ireland.[149]

Tensions consequent to the pervasive innuendoes of
English superiority to the Irish were treated by Catherine
in the "playful way" she recommended, knowing that
differences that could be laughed at would create bonds
of affectionate amusement, not barriers to mutual
appreciation.

In the process of establishing a spirit of community in
the Bermondsey foundation, Catherine, alert to the English sisters listening to catch her making "an Irish blun-
der," was quick to observe a quirk of language peculiar to
the English.[150] In response to an inquiry about her health,
Lady Barbara Ayre had replied, "a cold breaks one up so,"
a minute later adding "a cold breaks one down so," to
which Catherine commented: "We must suppose *up* and
down was all the same in her country."

Not to be outdone, the English sisters found great
amusement in Irish members voicing fears of "going
astray" or getting lost in unfamiliar neighborhoods, when
in England the expression "applied only to departure
from rectitude."

However, despite the ability to make light of differences, and despite the obvious appreciation for the personal qualities of Clare Moore who came to serve as
superior for the first year, Catherine recognized that the
truth of the human condition was such that in England:

Among the most amiable, we could clearly discover a desire that John Bull" should be the head
on all occasions.[151]

Aware that scenes foreign to Dublin and the other
Irish foundations held great interest back home,
Catherine drew vivid pictures for them from Bermondsey,
proving herself a master of description and reinforcing
the involvement she wanted all to feel with this effort to
establish the Sisters of Mercy in England.

The Bishop called the day we arrived. Wears a
gold chain and large cross outside his dress, and
purple stockings.[152]

The London bishop's exterior signs of office would
not have been customary in Ireland at that time. In
England, where pomp and pageantry were in style in polite
society, the insignia of the bishop was thought quite
proper and Catherine knew it would both intrigue and
amuse her readers.

Even while she regaled her readers with the lively accounts of foundation making, Catherine, sensitive to the
unspoken fears that Ireland would be found inferior to
England, reassured them with the observation, "I like the
Irish piety better."[153]

The convent in Bermondsey, the first built in England
since the Reformation, was a graceful Gothic-style building, designed by the renowned architect, Augustine
Pugin. Despite his prestige, Catherine felt free to
comment:

The convent is not more than half built, it is quite
in the old monastic style, very heavy. Mr. Pugin
the architect was determined we would not look
out of the windows, they are up to the ceiling. I
could not touch the glass without standing on a
chair. I do not admire his taste, though so
celebrated.[154]

Its ethereal Gothic was lost on her who wanted sisters
to see beyond the convent to the needs of the world. In the
midst of all the deference and adulation surrounding Irish
gentlewomen conquering London society, Catherine

never lost sight of what brought Sisters of Mercy to England:

There is great work here for the poor sisters—2 large Hospitals, Guy's and St. Thomas's; 4 work Houses; endless converts; the people delighted. You may judge how unceasingly we have been employed. Besides the spiritual and temporal preparation for the Sisters, we had to prepare dresses for 200 poor girls of the school who were to attend the ceremony.[155]

Chapter XI

AN INTEGRATED SPIRITUALITY

To have the official stamp of the Church remained a paramount concern for the Sisters of Mercy for whom the issue of acceptance was a debated one. Since they had "started up of themselves," and since they emerged from their convents to work among the poor, a practice foreign to communities of religious women, they caused as much alarm in some circles as benediction in others. Because they went out to perform works of mercy, staffed sectarian hospitals during epidemics, visited the sick poor in their homes, their status was a burning question.

In the mature wisdom characteristic of her, Catherine had recognized the necessity to submit the Rule they had drawn up to a trial period to discern if its prescriptions enabled them to fulfill lives of dedication to God in devoting their energies to the works of mercy. After five or six years of trial, she pronounced the Rule "well suited to our purpose,"[156] fitting both the devotional and apostolic aspirations of the congregation, and therefore sought final confirmation by Rome.

Because it would be a decided advantage in locations where bishops wished to introduce the Institute of Mercy into their dioceses for her sisters to arrive as a fully confirmed congregation, Catherine wrote:

Ecclesiastical authorities... are anxious to establish more Houses in England and in Ireland, which they think would be greatly facilitated by the full approbation of the Holy See, as all orders of the Clergy would then cooperate in promoting an order which they deem very conducive to the Interests of Religion.[157]

Catherine stressed the fact that the institute was a burgeoning one with great potential for the future:

When the petition was presented in December there were twelve Houses in full operation. We have since been added. One hundred forty-two Sisters are now devoted to God and His poor in this Order.[158]

Possessing a hard-won faith, Catherine desired to have the blessing of the Church on her work, a Church she understood as servant, carrying on the mission of Christ seeking to serve the world. In this she anticipated modern theological and ecclesiological frameworks that help to interpret and validate her charism, her intuition and inspiration.

Catherine McAuley was not content that her institute merely attend to the social ills pervading her society. She was impelled to affect the spirit, the innerlife, that flashes out like "shining from shook foil." Her grasp of the presence of God in the most wretched person allowed her to see that the poverty, sickness, and ignorance which prevent the spirit of a person from shining through were enemies to be overcome so that the divine spark would inform all of life ever more brightly.

Union and Charity

That this reverence for each one whose life they touched was rooted in the love and respect of the members for one another is clearly evident in Catherine's shaping of the Rule. To her question at the inception of the Institute of Mercy, "What shall we use as a Rule?", the archbishop had answered simply, "The Chapter on Union and Charity in the Rule of the Presentation Sisters."

Interpreted by Catherine, this chapter gave focus to their spirituality, demanding that each respect and reverence another's gifts, talents, and disposition, as well as accept each individual's physical, emotional, psychic, and spiritual limitations. It created unity within variety by permitting members to retain their own personalities while becoming bonded as Sisters of Mercy.

In general, eighteenth and nineteenth century piety emphasized an individual's relationship with God. Even exhortations to the practice of virtue could seem to make another a function of one's own advancement in grace. Catherine's emphasis on union and charity asked more than functional unity. Her sense of union had to do with a love that generated concern for each person. Members of the new institute were to learn to love one another, to appreciate one another's contribution, to believe in one another's good intentions and desires. From these attitudes, Sisters of Mercy could hope to become forgiving and reconciling presences not just to one another, but to those who worked with them, and to those whom they served. When Catherine reflected on the outstanding characteristic of their lives and work together, a spontaneous description emerged of the source of their strength and compassion.

> One thing is remarkable, that no breach of charity ever occurred amongst us. The Sun never, I believe, went down on our anger. This is our only boast, otherwise we have been deficient enough, and far, very far from cooperating generously with God in our regard, but we will try to do better, all of us.[159]

Nothing in Catherine's makeup permitted her to be boastful, to exaggerate, or to dissemble. That she stated matter-of-factly, "This is our only boast," and followed it with the admission that they would lay claim to no other similar response to the grace of God, charged her assertion with truthfulness. The precious heritage of the early days of the founding community was one of union and charity cherished and practiced with fidelity.

Catherine did not claim that they were never angry with one another. She claimed rather that the sun never set on that anger. The truth of her assertion can be further realized by the spontaneous fun and laughter that dominated their gatherings, by light-hearted verses sent back and forth, and by the lack of formality evident in the cordiality of their relationships.

The letters reflect the good-humored teasing and playful repartee that was exchanged among them, revealing the affectionate regard that characterized their lives together. Whether the message was a fond assurance that "Dr.' Warde's prescription shall be carefully followed,"[160] a mildly deprecatory note that "Fr.' McAuley conducts the retreat,"[161] or a facetious reference to Sister Mary Anne Doyle as "her Reverence,"[162] the tone of affection is clear.

Whether in spontaneous letters, in playful verse, or in more considered writings, Catherine's concern for safeguarding the nature of the Institute of Mercy is seen in the responsibility she took for developing its character and spirit as well as its works. Her letters reveal this felt sense of responsibility for guiding foundation development and for supporting sisters whose formation she had begun. Catherine registered how seriously she took the command of Jesus at the Last Supper for his followers to live in union with him, with the Father, and with each other. Pouring forth her vision, she named these cordial, open relationships the spirit of the order.

> All are good and happy. The blessing of unity still dwells amongst us and oh what a blessing, it should make all things else pass into nothing. All laugh and play together, not one cold, stiff soul appears. From the day they enter, all reserve of any ungracious kind leaves them. This is the spirit of the Order, indeed the true spirit of Mercy flowing on us, that notwithstanding our unworthiness God never seems to visit us with angry punishment. He may punish a little in mercy, but never in wrath. Take what He will from us, He still leaves His holy peace, and this He has graciously extended to all our convents.[163]

Catherine had a deep faith that the spirit of unity was God's gift par excellence. Angry punishments were those that resulted in divisions or factions, and in lesser degree in petty jealousies, unkindness, and coldness. Where these existed, Catherine believed that the withdrawal of God's enabling power or grace became his angry punishment. Offenses proceeding from inherited disposition, weakness, or as yet unreformed habits did not impede union in charity. These everyday happenings provided opportunities for developing compassion, forgiveness, and healing reconciliations. These increased the bond of mutual charity.

The peace Catherine rejoiced in was that peace which proceeds from loving acceptance of one another's gifts and weaknesses. In the midst of all her concerns for foundations abroad, at home, and for Baggot Street itself, she had the vision to name the sign of the institute's spiritual health, strength, and future endurance as well as to name its lifegiving charism. Out of a loving, forgiving union with one another and out of the learnings that ensue from ongoing reconciliations, Sisters of Mercy would be enabled for compassionate service to others, for mercy is but the overflow of charity.

A letter titled "An Introductory Meditation' written to Sister Mary Delamere, a postulant in Tullamore, shows Catherine's determination to create a relaxed climate of community life and to eliminate any legalism or artifice which would engender an atmosphere of rigidity or diminish the affective quality of relationships.

Preparing the most likely member of the local foundation for her visit, Catherine wrote playfully of her expectations of a week of folly. In announcing the companions who would accompany her, Catherine assessed whether she could hope they would support her plan:

> I fear Sister Mary Clare will join the "Divine Mother". She is rather too good for my taste. Sister Catherine is according to our own heart, and surely Sister Eliza will not desert us. If Mrs. Doyle should complain to the Bishop—remember you and I are safe we are not of his flock—most fortunately.[164]

To encourage Mary Delamere to join her in pursuing this lightsome spirit of fun, Catherine explained that the local pastor would find her plot and plan very agreeable as sound doctrine.

> I know very well Father Murtagh will applaud our pious intention, for such it really is, when rightly considered. First, it will effectually remove all the painful remembrance of our former separation and animate us to go through a second parting. It will show superiors and their assistants

that it is necessary sometimes to yield to the inclinations of others, and convince them that authority, however good, cannot always last. It
also affords them an opportunity, if they will
take advantage of it, of seeing dispositions and
manners that might remain unknown to them,
and consequently unchanged.

While obliquely commenting on the self-conscious
gravity and formality sometimes assumed by religious
persons as the proper mark of consecration, a formality
to which Mary Anne Doyle was inclined, Catherine emphasized her conviction that, for teaching to be effective, desired behaviors must be "modeled." Repeatedly her
letters urge her first associate to teach "by example more
than precept."[165]

More than just a graceful, charming, well-educated
lady, Catherine was a woman with a deeply motivated love
for others. She planned to model open and fun-loving behaviors she realized others might never have experienced
and therefore could not cultivate. For Catherine, the en-
joyment of being together in community was one of the re-
inforcements and supports needed to carry on the hard,
often dreary work that filled the days of a Sister of Mercy.

Her long schooling in the charity of courtesy gave her
both self-possession and liberty of action. Not chained
herself by artificial formalized responses, Catherine evidently had misgivings that the sisters in Tullamore had
not acquired such personal liberty of spirit. Her comment
underscored her concern and she therefore resolved to
spend the time spontaneously, freely, joyfully in order to
present the model she would have imitated.

We must banish all these visionary matters with
laughing notes, with hop-step for the ceremony,
to be concluded with 'The Lady of Flesh and
Bone.' We will set up what I will call a Nonsensi-
cal Club. I will be President, you Vice-president,
and Catherine can give lectures as Professor of
Folly.[166]

Catherine's belief that persons drew motivations
from what they experienced in others underpinned her insistence that sisters model whatever they wanted another

to learn. Because she feared that the atmosphere in Tullamore might be too stiff and formal for her liking, she brought with her an entourage of lively sisters from Baggot Street to visit those whose experience she wished to broaden. Catherine's advance notice announcing that she intended to demonstrate a cheerful gaiety which she desired as the hallmark of community relationships explained a strategy to display spontaneous and affectionate relationships so that those who had not experienced that style of religious living could adopt manners formerly not recognized as proper to their state.

Playfully, Catherine warned, "The good Mother Superior will not have equal reason to rejoice, for I am determined not to behave well, and you must join me." She did not want convent life to be lived with grim seriousness. Determined to evidence lightsome ways of handling oneself that added charm and amiability to human relationships, she registered concern that an over-regard for regularity, an over-emphasis on the dignity of the religious state, as well as too much insistence on formality were developing at Tullamore.

In fairness to Mary Anne Doyle, it must be realized that she was only twenty-six years old and had the responsibility of being the first founding superior after Catherine McAuley herself. Her exactness in observation of the Rule can be easily understood.

Although fun-loving, specious arguments heralded the lightheartedness Catherine desired to exist among the Tullamore community, after outlining her scheme for the week of Folly, warm affection took over in her closing paragraphs.

One thing, however, I am sure and seriously so, that I seldom look forward to any change in this world with such happiness as I do to our meeting.

A later request to Mary Anne Doyle for hospitality en route to Birr evoked a response that Catherine was eager to share with the community since it afforded a glimpse of the winsome side of the "Divine Mother" whose reputation would remain one of dignified reserve, grave demeanor, and piety.

Catherine had asked that Mary Ann answer "quickly, plainly, and briefly." Her entertaining response, graceful and lighthearted, surprised those to whom Catherine read it, since in the Birr superior's words, "She did not suppose there was so much life in that quarter!"

> *Cead mille Failthe.* Good day's lodgings, entertainment for man and beast, coffee for teetotalers, Mass at 8 o'c. Breakfast 9:30, visit to New Convent at 10. 2 first-rate chaises from Head Inn at the door at 12. Refreshments with PP of English (Father Murtaugh) half way. Arrive in Birr 4 o'c p.m. No fog until 5. Dear Rev. Mother approach![167]

That Catherine quoted the message in a letter to Elizabeth Moore indicates her delight in the spirit of fun and affectionate regard it contained.

Light-hearted verses written back and forth between Catherine and her community also witness the lively, friendly interchange which characterized their life together and, at the same time, reveal the superior gently urging her sisters toward the ideals she held out to them.

Sister Francis Marmion, a novice in charge of the sick poor at Baggot Street, had received a half crown from a visitor. In her seeking permission to use the money for the poor, an exchange of poems shows Catherine holding out the ideal to a young novice, using a playful tone which makes her point while yielding to the petitioner's request.

> To my great surprise, you demanded last night
> The enclosed as your own, your particular right.
> I am sorry to find such a matter distract you
> I did not suppose such a crown would attract you
> But since with reluctance from it you would part
> Take it—there is no such tie on my heart.

Not in the least perturbed by Catherine's pointed acquiescence to her request, Frances' spirited response in the same candid, easy tone, testifies to the mutual understanding which existed.

> Dear Mother, in spite of your jesting, I own
> That I ever ambitiously sigh for a crown
> Which the one you surrender may aid me to gain

And therefore the right of my poor I maintain.
This very day twelvemonth it was, that you bound
With black leather cincture my waist and will round
And to tell of my happiness humbly I pray
That the Sisters may have recreation today.

Catherine's rejoinder maintained the familial spirit, making a feigned allowance for the youth of her community.

I rejoice in your motive for liking this day
Though not in wishing to spend it in play
I must freely confess it were more to my mind
If to reflection your heart were inclined,
But since you're not weaned, nor alone cannot walk
I suppose you must do what you can do, then talk.

To understand these scenes, it is necessary to put them against the backdrop of unremitting toil among the poor, with much of it in very squalid quarters. If these women did not find innocent pleasure to divert them, heaviness would have been all consuming. The evening's recreation afforded easy release in spontaneous fun-making and eager sharing of the daily events that make up any group's lived history.

The same woman who claimed that the blessing of unity still dwelt among them understood human nature. She could assert that no breach of charity ever occurred among them, and yet advise that none should be "surprised that anyone dare say what you dare do."[168] Commenting on the death of Sister Gertrude Jones, a stolid and stoic convert, Catherine remarked that she "fancied all who faithfully observed [the Catholic faith] must be divine, hence she was disappointed."[169] Catherine had no such illusions; she held out to her community the ideal of striving with fidelity to "be good today, but better tomorrow,"[170] understanding that holiness could be achieved only in the constant and unwearied struggle of becoming.

Apostolic Spirituality

With a shared vision, Catherine and her first associates had so unequivocally reduced their Rule to practice before submitting it for approval that the bishop of Cork urged at a profession in 1837 that they add a fourth vow—the service of the poor, the sick, and the ignorant—as both integral to their dedication and descriptive of it.

Catherine's conviction that the works of mercy were the very "business of our lives,"[171] had shaped the community from its inception in an apostolic spirituality. She had emphasized this spirituality in retreat conferences to the sisters at Baggot Street: "Prayer, retirement, and recollection are not sufficient for those called to labor for the salvation of souls [They should be like] the compass that goes round its circle without stirring from its center. Now, our center is God from Whom all our actions should spring as from their source, and no exterior action should separate us from Him."[172]

To go out to the poor, the sick, the ignorant was not to leave an atmosphere of prayer. As she moved from one foundation to another, Catherine noted the spirit which motivated the activity.

> We have one solid comfort amidst this little tripping about, our hearts can always be in the same place, centered in God, for whom alone we go forward or stay back.[173]

While it is familiar to hear in the post-Vatican II Church that a spirituality based on reading "the signs of the times" requires, instead of oblivion of the world, an asceticism of awareness, discernment, courage, and response, Catherine suffered because her vision was not widely accepted by her contemporaries.

Since the "walking nuns" were held under some suspicion by both clergy and laity in Dublin society as not being proper religious, a penchant to take on practices of the ascetical life arose in some members of the new order. This struggle to become "proper religious" continued for many years and is reflected in the annals of Carlow, Wexford, and Bermondsey. Catherine's letters made several references to her concern that there was in some convents too much emphasis on rigor, fasting, and formalized life styles.

With wisdom and balance, she asserted the value of prayer and contemplation, and the importance of a profound inner life, while insisting at the same time that in service of God's people, works unite us to God.

The troubles that arose at Baggot Street during Catherine's absence while at George's Hill give evidence of the disparity from her vision. As each one "mismanaged her spiritualities in her own way,"[174] such practices as imprudent fasting, sleeping in haircloth, and praying all night show the type of religious spirit against which Catherine had to fight.

As the young community developed, two visions of religious life grew side by side, one emphasizing a contemplative spirituality and one the active life. Ascetical practices common to cloistered communities appealed to Mary Anne Doyle's sense of religious devotion; Catherine grasped and taught the asceticism of compassionate service, discouraging not only those practices which would render sisters being "incapable of the duties of the Institute,"[175] but any which would diminish the quality of their service.

Mary Anne Doyle had been educated in convent boarding schools and was attracted to those pieties which contributed to the mystique of religious life. Catherine McAuley, in contrast, had been "personally acquainted with few Catholics"[176], and found convent customs "particularly distasteful."[177] This contrast in their backgrounds helps to explain their differing perceptions of practices appropriate to a religious community.

As superior in Tullamore, Mary Anne would be fondly dubbed "Her Reverence," or "The Divine Mother"; Catherine, noted for protesting against signs of deference, had "a total absence of everything in her manner telling 'I am the Foundress,'"[178] and desire "not to have the title of Mother amongst us,"[179] acquiescing to this formality only at the insistence of Archbishop Murray.

The monastic austerity to which Mary Anne was inclined and the cheerful practicality of Catherine are caught in a description of the convent rooms in Tullamore:

> Mother Mary Ann has met with her "beau ideal"
> of a conventual building at last, for our rooms are
> so small, that two cats could scarcely dance in

them. The rest of us however would have no objection to larger ones.[180]

The ongoing tension inherent in these two perspectives is reflected in annals which record discussions among novices as to whether or not they were "proper" religious. Convinced "that sanctity could be acquired in the exercise of the contemplative life only,"[181] they compared themselves to other congregations and found them more "holy."

For Catherine, who had insisted from the beginning on freedom from cloister, holiness was bound up with works of mercy. For her, spirituality was not the multiplication of prayers and practices, but the lived experience of faith, the action of God in her daily life and her graced response.

Encouraging thoughtful behaviors that avoided all pious affectations, she especially rejected the practice of downcast eyes, "for this might give some persons a rather disagreeable expression of countenance. The countenance should be always modest and ever pleasing to behold."[182] Writing to Frances Warde after interviewing a candidate who had spent six months in a Carmelite convent, Catherine, in an almost audible sigh, laments the task she will have in "opening the eyes of the little Carmelite," who had indeed acquired "the holy art of keeping custody of eyes, for she seldom opens them."[183]

With a wisdom that understood that excessive rigidity or formalism impedes psychological health, Catherine did not hesitate to declare that there will be "no more improvements while I live"[184] when she observed being introduced into the Baggot Street novitiate by Cecilia Marmion who had come under the influence of Clare Agnew while accompanying Catherine during the Bermondsey foundation.

This apostolic/contemplative tension reached its climax when Clare Agnew, whom Catherine had noted was "fond of *extremes* in piety,"[185] took over as superior in Bermondsey. The extremes exceeded Catherine's wildest imagination as Clare Agnew initiated such bizarre customs as having the community sit facing the wall during meals as an aid to recollection or requiring those of short stature to stand on boxes during spiritual exercise in choir to maintain an orderly appearance. It was not long before she announced, contrary to the stipulation in the recently approved Rule that "the daily duties are the same for all," that the members of the Bermondsey community might choose between active and contemplative life. Finally, "believ[ing] she was favored... with supernatural revelations and visions... directing her to establish Perpetual Adoration in the Community,"[186] Clare Agnew petitioned the bishop for this permission.[187]

When word of this inclination toward the extreme cloister of contemplative life, a proclivity which would destroy the essential thrust of the Sisters of Mercy—the ability to go beyond convent gates in the service of the poor, the sick, and the ignorant—reached Catherine, she steered herself and her institute through the dilemma of choosing between apparent antithetical realities in a document known as the "Spirit of the Institute,"[188] a vigorous defense of the spirituality of active religious life.

Possessed of a conviction that prayer should never withdraw Sisters of Mercy from works of mercy but rather enkindle their hearts with enthusiasm for service, she used Scripture, spiritual teachers, and reflection on contemporary images to explain the inextricable link between the spirit of prayer and the "business of our lives," the corporal and spiritual works of mercy.

Catherine had noted in a letter that "the perpetual movements of the steam train carriages which do not cease from morning till night" are an example of the "power [persons] possess of exercising unwearied efforts of body and mind," an image she found apt.[189] For her, the constant stoking of the fire needed to keep the carriages in "perpetual movement" mirrored the life of the active religious in that religious and apostolic aspects are inseparable and mutually compenetrated.

The habit of reflection that Catherine McAuley achieved was not simply a practice of guarding exterior senses, cultivating the mind to think above and beyond present duties. This view appraised human tasks as necessary but secondary. As such they were understood to interfere with the primary or spiritual obligation or exercises. Catherine had learned how to utilize the activities of each hour to be the matter of her reflection, and never accepted a contemplative/apostolic dichotomy. She insisted that active works must be done without losing awareness of the presence of God, convinced that the Sister of Mercy must make mission the ambience of her recollection, as she makes charity the ambience and quality of her service.

Cross and Crown

Catherine's ability to reflect on her experiences taught her the rhythms of light and darkness, of pain and surcease, of sorrow and joy, of death and resurrection, or of "cross and crown." She had tremendous confidence that one would follow the other with regularity, and taught that a life of peace and harmony was to be achieved from the constant integration of these paradoxical realities.

Possessing a lived understanding of the Paschal Mystery, she used the language of "cross and crown," seeing sufferings at work in her life and in the life of the institute as ways of taking up the cross and dying daily to self to resurrect the spirit and to grow in greater union with God.

Catherine's deepest theology consisted in her belief that the cross was part of life. To embrace it released new and creative powers from suffering, pain, and death. She believed sorrows were to be felt, yet transcended through the free choice to yield—learning through yielding the lesson of the seed's dying to come to new life. Everything in life had the power to ennoble and transform, for "without the Cross the real Crown cannot come."[190]

To grasp the significance of Catherine's assertion, "Without the Cross, the real Crown cannot come," it must be understood as springing from her deep prayer, her personal experience of suffering, her study of the life of Christ, her experiences of the effect of sufferings in her own life and in the lives of others.

Catherine had experienced herself in the hand of a loving God, carved in the palm of his hand. She knew that the mysteries of life were indeed inscrutable but believed that the paradigm of the Passion and Death and Resurrection was at work in the lives of his people.

One of the most difficult trials Catherine had to endure resulted from her conviction that the chapel at Baggot Street should have one official chaplain. Father Armstrong—friend, confidant, and pastor of Westland Row when the house on Baggot Street was being built— had strongly recommended that one chaplain should serve them. Although the archbishop had appointed Fr. Daniel Burke chaplain on the dedication of the chapel in 1829, the departure of this Franciscan for the African missions eight years later resulted in Catherine's becoming embroiled in a difficult struggle with the parish priest, Dr. Walter Meyler, who preferred that the three curates would share this ministry among them.

Catherine would not accept a shared-chaplaincy to the Convent and House of Mercy, and Dr. Meyler, pastor of St. Andrew's, would not appoint an individual chaplain. Neither would yield.

Busy with the establishment of the Cork foundation during October of 1837, Catherine delegated the handling of this dispute to her assistant, Sister de Pazzi, arming her with her persistent argument that Mr. Armstrong had engraved an objection "not to be overruled." The precise reason for the objection remained uncommunicated. It was a private caution and Catherine kept it that way.

In her discernment of the situation, Catherine viewed herself as being faithful to the injunction of her first advisor and protector, Dr. Armstrong. Dr. Meyler's assessment was that Catherine was being willful and stubborn not to accept the services of the parish curates whose schedules he would set.

No one who succeeds to an office or responsibility wants to be told how the predecessor did things more wisely or more fairly. The intrusion of the memory of the former pastor proved a blind spot for both of them, exacerbating the disagreement over the assignment of a chaplain to the chapel. Catherine, unaffected in her manner, was not prepared for the sophisticated sarcasm of Walter Meyler's assertion: "I feel Dr. Armstrong pushing me to make these arrangements,"[191] as his retort to her insistence that her requirement was based on the strong advice of her friend. The very mention of Dr. Armstrong's name prompted Catherine to wax eloquent as to how the kindly Edward Armstrong had dealt with the religious women under his care in contradistinction to Dr. Meyler's stringent dealings with the House of Mercy.

Although the long-standing animus of Dr. Meyler toward Catherine and the House of Mercy likely influenced his determination not to yield on this issue, it is clear that financial arrangements were also a factor. Catherine noted that, even if she could agree to his proposal of the curates sharing the chaplaincy, he required "£50 per annum, which we really have not, independent of casual events."[192]

A letter of advice from Dr. Blake lends support to the financial aspect of the difficulty.

> It appears to me from your letter that our worthy friend, Dr. Meyler, is not absolutely opposed to your having a distinct chaplain, and that his objection rests on the persuasion that the salary you could afford for the support of a chaplain would be insufficient and that, therefore, it would be for the advantage of your Community to have the duty of chaplain performed by a curate of the parish.[193]

Since it was a matter of principle for her not to accept "at least three priests," Catherine examined the results of her actions with a criteria of discernment that seems to have had an Ignatian base.

> We have just now indeed more than an ordinary portion of the Cross in this one particular, but may it not be the Cross of Christ which we so often pray to be about us. It has not the marks of an angry Cross, there is no disunion, no gloomy depression of spirits, no departure from charity proceeding from it.[194]

Reassuring Frances about the situation, Catherine protested that she was not unduly burdened, certain that no understanding of the proportions of the controversy had reached the public.

> I am not unhappy, thanks be to God, nor do I see any disedification likely to arise from the matter. Some think that after having Mr. Burke eight years, we are not now easily pleased and most of those who know the cause that we go out seem to think we ought to have a distinct chaplain, and only say Dr. Meyler is a little positive.

While Catherine could maintain a light heart, assuring Frances Warde that going to Westland Row every morning "gives a very good appetite for our breakfast,"[195] her real suffering of the consequences of the dispute emerges in her letter to the archdiocese:

> Even a friendly priest is not permitted to celebrate Mass—... the Blessed Eucharist has not been renewed for near three months,... the poor inmates are deprived of the Holy Sacraments.[196]

Catherine felt the obligation not to occasion an attack on or denouncement of another, especially a priest of the Church, but continued to appeal to every quarter open to her for help. Her letters to the chancery of the Dublin archdiocese describe her bitter sufferings, her direct and simple attempt to clear up the controversy, and her blind spot as to what she did to anger Dr. Meyler.

Correspondence from her long-time friend and advisor, Dr. Michael Blake, who had been parish priest at St. Andrew's prior to Dean Meyler gives insight into the compromise that was eventually reached. Dr. Blake suggested that the appointment of a curate as chaplain would alleviate the financial burden at Baggot Street, and that Dean Meyler most likely required the salary stipulated so that in arranging with one of his curates he could use the salary as "a conditional bond for an exact fulfillment of the duties for which it is given."[197]

That Dr. Meyler's adherence to his original proposal was not absolute is clear in an undated letter to Catherine.

> Have not the least doubt of the advantages of this arrangement both to the House of Mercy and to the Parish.
>
> If it should appear otherwise—after the sermon and a sufficient trial, new regulations can be made. When the time of the Charity Sermon will draw near I shall afford you every assistance in my power and beg that you will enroll me as an annual subscriber of £5 – which I shall remit in a few days.[198]

In an eventual compromise, Dr. Meyler agreed to name one of his curates responsible, and Catherine increased the salary.

To their credit, neither permitted the dispute to become public. Elizabeth Moore understood the tension between Dr. Meyler and Catherine over his refusal to appoint a single chaplain to the House of Mercy. She therefore could appreciate the description of the controlled performances both gave at a dinner following a reception ceremony.

> Sisters Fleming and Whitty, two very nice persons not twenty-one... were received yesterday by Dean Meyler, gracious as possible. Mrs. McA a very good child, smiling and praying alternately, attended at table and paid great attention to.[199]

That Catherine found it necessary to smile and pray alternately communicated the anxiety hidden under her tranquil deportment. Welcoming her adversary as the honored guest of the occasion called up a lifetime's good breeding. As Dr. Meyler was "gracious as possible," they were evidently both on their best behavior. Not simply a surface art, Catherine's courtesy proved itself especially under attack or duress.

Anticipating the closing of the Kingstown convent, Catherine agreed to a request from neighboring Booterstown to establish a Convent of Mercy there. Writing a long letter to Frances Warde describing the convent, Catherine—as if she were whispering about the effects of the external pressures on her—opened her heart to Frances.

> We are in the very midst of the Sandymount Patronesses, and feel it.[200]

These supporters of the Sisters of Charity, who from the earliest moments of Baggot Street were opposed to the "competition" they saw in the new religious group, reopened Catherine's wounds, forcing her to deal anew with the feeling of resentment. Anyone who befriended them, no matter how important, was cut socially, adding another complexity to her own response. She confided to Frances, "Dr. Murphy [Bishop of Cork] is cast off."

In Catherine's response, it is clear that she felt the need of spiritual help to restore peace and equanimity.

Pray fervently to God to take all bitterness from me. I can scarcely think of what has been done to me without resentment. May God forgive me and make me humble before He calls me into His Presence.

Placed in the context of her comment on the Sandymount patronesses, this reference suggests that she experienced her difficulties in both the chaplaincy dispute and the Kingstown controversy, which may have been aided and abetted by these stalwart opponents, who no doubt considered Catherine their social inferior.

In the midst of her trials with the respective clergymen in the Kingstown and chaplaincy disputes, trials which were exacerbated by the internal stress of sickness, death, and differing perceptions of religious propriety, Catherine acknowledged the support and encouragement she received from other clergy. After a visit to Carlow, she asked Frances to remember her especially to Dr. Fitzgerald "who has taken such a kind feeling part in my troubles" and

...most gratefully to the other good clergymen from whom we experienced such attention; Mr. Raftee, Mr. Taylor, Mr. McCarthy, etc., etc. and Father Dan. To Mr. Maher, you could not omit to offer my grateful remembrance.[201]

Catherine relished loyal friendship but especially that of Dr. Andrew Fitzgerald, president of Carlow College.

Dr. Fitzgerald proclaimed privately and publicly against what he conceived unjust and unkind. Indeed he gave me great comfort for while he condemned the proceeding, he reasoned with me so as to produce quiet of mind and heart.[202]

As important to her as obtaining justice was the ability to live with a "quiet mind and heart" toward decisions she could neither affect nor change. Anyone who could help her deepen this response was friend indeed.

That Catherine suffered moments of depression is evident; that she was able to transcend them is illustrated in the perspective she was able to keep on the Kingstown difficulty. Having felt the injustice of being deceived, she, nevertheless, could see the humor in her hiding from the sheriff, and entertained Frances with an account of the general amusement occasioned by the efforts at Baggot Street to protect her from being served process papers.

> I am hiding from some law person who wants to serve a paper on me personally, and sent in to say he came from Dr. Murray. I am afraid to remain five minutes in the small parlor. This has caused more laughing than crying, you may be sure, for every man is suspected of being the process man, and kept at an awful distance by my dear Teresa Carton.[203]

At the same time, aware that she would probably lose the legal battle, her strong sense of the Paschal Mystery at work in painful events enabled her to reassure Frances that out of these sufferings God's blessings were experienced among them.

> I suppose we must sell Kingstown.... Now you have the double cross, the cross of the diocese— out of it—all is consoling and animating, thanks be to God.

The crisis came to a head a short time later while Catherine was in Limerick, ending in the removal of the Sisters of Mercy from Kingstown. Because these misunderstandings dug so deeply into Catherine, she was doubly grateful for the tact and diplomacy with which Teresa White conducted the sensitive withdrawal.

> How can I sufficiently thank you for the kind cautious manner in which you communicated the painful news....

Because only a one-sided correspondence exists, Teresa White's letter has to be extrapolated as one in which she mourned the withdrawal as detrimental to the poor. To comfort Teresa as well as to set forth her own position clearly, Catherine urged Teresa to accept what was happening with faith in the mysterious workings of God in the lives of those who serve him.

We have done all that justice and prudence demand to avert this affliction. If it must be done, let us receive it as the Holy Will of God in our regard. It will mortify us and that will be salutary, please God. . . . Be a good soldier in the hour of trial. Do not be afflicted for your poor, their Heavenly Father will provide comfort for them, and you will have the same opportunity of fulfilling your obligations during your life.[204]

Catherine could assert her faith-filled confidence that God was present even in the midst of such anxiety.

I feel that it would give you no consolation were I to say: "God would not be displeased with you, though He may with me." He will not be displeased with me, for He knows I would rather be cold and hungry than the poor in Kingstown or elsewhere should be deprived of any consolation in our power to afford. But in the present case, we have done all that belonged to us to do, and even more than the circumstances justified.

Submission to the inevitable in life is requisite for all willing to live in peace with mystery. Submission can be servile—hardly a proper stance for children of a loving Father, as Catherine taught:

Submit we must, but we should do much more, we should praise and bless the hand that wounds us, and exhibit to all around us a calm quiet appearance and manner.[205]

When Catherine received word that the Limerick foundation was experiencing its first death, she drew upon her confidence in God to send the community a message of peace and hope to root them in faith in the goodness of God.

This has not been done in anger. Some joyful circumstance will soon prove that God is watching over your concerns, which are all His own, but without the Cross the real Crown cannot come. Some great thing which He designs to accomplish would have been too much without a little bitter in the cup. Bless and love the fatherly Hand which has hurt you. He will soon come with both Hands filled with favors and blessings.[206]

Catherine's faith, nourished by a theology that accepts readily the truth that God does indeed intervene in his creatures' lives, demanded that God's intervening be welcomed externally as well as internally. What God sent or permitted might indeed be very costly to an individual, but joining in the event with the intervening Lord allowed little room for indulging whatever suffering was involved.

Throughout her letters, Catherine refers to specific moments of encounter with the cross. Her confidence in its victory increased from year to year as she recorded the afflictions she endured within her own life as well as those she endured through suffering with others. Whether it was the pain of loss of young and valued members of the institute, painful human relations, or the pain of her own deteriorating health, the gentle courage and calm with which she bore all veiled their intensity.

In the advice or counsel she gave to others, she revealed the Paschal Mystery as the deepest food for her spirit. She had experienced its transforming work in the recesses of her soul and taught from that experience, welcoming difficulties that could not be surmounted as a share of the cross of Christ. Receiving these sorrows from the hand of a loving God, Catherine believed that whatever came from this source would ultimately become a blessing in her own life and in the life of the institute. Often burnished as gold in the fire, she seemed to come forth more enthusiastic, more compassionate, more joyful, more possessed by God.

When she wrote to Frances Warde, telling her of some effects of sickness at Baggot Street and the on-going chaplaincy and Kingstown disputes, she commented:

> Thus we go on. . . flourishing in the very midst of the Cross, more than a common share of which has lately fallen to my lot, thanks be to God. I humbly trust it is the Cross of Christ.[207]

Catherine's deepest sufferings lay in the loss of sisters who succumbed to the diseases prevalent in the early nineteenth century. She felt each one's death keenly, mourning in each the loss of friend, of one gathered with her by God's call, of her sister in mercy. Tending many of them in the throes of fatal illness, she suffered without hardening her heart against the pain of life or becoming insensitive and inattentive to the sufferers.

Nevertheless, when Catherine wrote to Dr. Fitzgerald to tell him of the death of her niece Catherine, only one who knew that she spoke of a niece for whom she was legal guardian, devoted aunt, and second mother would realize her personal anguish. Catherine's spirituality required her to lay no greater claim of loss than others in the community might feel. Aware of the sorrow of all around her, she identified her pain with theirs and shared in their grief.

> Our innocent little Catherine is out of this miserable world. . . . We feel just now as if all the House was dead. All are sorry to part with our animated, sweet little companion.[208]

Never finding it easy to send "out of this miserable world" anyone she loved, Catherine put aside her personal grief in a simple statement, "Thank God it is over."

While Catherine worried over the sick and anguished over those lost to death, she experienced particular anxieties whenever she found a lack of religious spirit manifesting itself. So strong was her grasp that God and each human person are in constant partnership to reveal the Father's wisdom, power, and goodness that it distressed her when anyone acted as if good accomplished depended on the individual person. Catherine had brought Teresa Carton to Booterstown for "change of air," relieving her of her duty of supervising the Baggot Street children who carried letters of solicitation to the wealthy. Teresa alarmed Catherine by the degree of possessiveness she revealed toward directing the activity.

> She distressed me very much yesterday. I almost thought she was sorry to hear the collection children went on as usual. Perhaps I was mistaken. Please God she will triumph over this human weakness, and I rejoice at the good which must result from her seeing that those things do

not depend on anyone in particular but on the continuance of God's blessing.[209]

Catherine, willing to doubt her own perceptions, was not willing that she or any of her sisters should think of themselves as the necessary ingredient to whatever good was accomplished nor think of any work as their own. Her use of *Please God* was a very deliberate prayer to deepen Teresa's faith.

Out of her understanding of the cross in the life of the institute, Catherine—always affected more by the sufferings of others than by her own—entered into Frances Warde's distress over a sister who withdrew from Carlow.

How deeply, how sincerely, I feel this second trial which it has pleased almighty God to visit you with, not in His anger, we will humbly hope, but to purify and render the foundation solid and according to His own Heart, established on the Cross.[210]

Catherine called Frances to overcome her grief and bring forth the gifts she had within her.

You have given all to God without any reserve. Nothing can happen to you which He does not appoint. You desire nothing but the accomplishment of His holy will. Everything, how trivial soever, regarding you will come from this adorable Source. You must be cheerful and happy, animating all around you.[211]

Strong faith in the power of God to make everything work unto good lay behind Catherine's deep desires for Frances to be stretched to new dimensions of herself.

This is quite unnecessary, for I know you do not want counsel or comfort, yet I cannot entirely give up my poor old child. You may be sure we all pray fervently for you, which is the best we can do.... You will soon now have an increase. The comfort comes soon after a well-received trial.

Ever alert to circumstances which might pain her sisters, and having heard that a clerical reappointment in Carlow had removed Frances Warde's spiritual director and friend, Catherine reiterated her belief in the rhythms of the spiritual life.

> I know it is an affliction to you, but rest assured, God will send some distinguished consolation. This is your life, joys and sorrows mingled, one succeeding the other.[212]

Catherine's spiritual vision put no blame upon human instruments for the pain, sufferings, or deprivations that entered her life. In imitation of Jesus, what God permitted, she accepted. Whatever happened came from him directly or indirectly. Whatever way, to love him was to welcome the painful, difficult, sorrowful, or suffering moment.

> Let us not think of the means employed to convey to us a portion of the holy Cross, being ever mindful that it came from Himself.[213]

She recalled for Frances the words of a retreat master concerning the welcoming of God in all events, especially difficult ones.

> You remember what Father Gaffney said to us when in Retreat: If the entire Cross upon which Christ died was sent to the House, how impatient would each Sister be to carry it, and she who was permitted to keep it the longest would be the most favored. Far better and more profitable for you to receive with all your heart the Cross which God will send you in any form or shape He pleases."[214]

The pattern of the mystery of the cross unfolded again and again for Catherine. Even in her most spontaneous outpourings, she could not encompass an expectation that life should be without trials, sorrows, anxieties. She desired that they not come too soon to her beloved sisters. She knew they would come and she knew too the transcendence they could give to those who made surrender a choice.

The acceptance in faith of events one cannot control was an asceticism for Catherine, not an attitude which came easily to her. Sorely tried by the fact that no date had been set for the profession ceremony for the Birmingham sisters, she was annoyed that departure plans for England remained uncertain as a result. The impatience which poured out spontaneously was retracted in the same sentence.

No time appointed for our ceremony yet— perplexed with disappointment, I ought to say delighted—the bad spirit spoke first.[215]

Catherine could not help judging that a "bad spirit" animated her when she was "perplexed with disappointment." To her it was tarnish on her confidence in God. The promise of an English bishop's appearance at the Baggot Street ceremony had caused ripples of excitement to roll over Dublin society. Many inquiries were being made by those anxious to attend. English visitors had arrived and had taken lodgings in Dublin in order to be present whenever the ceremony took place. Catherine had reason to feel perplexed and disappointed.

She had helped the Birmingham novices compose a letter of invitation to Bishop Walsh to attend their profession and to receive personally the vows of his English spiritual daughters. Since Bishop Walsh's acceptance involved the courtesy of permitting him to set the date, all preparations had to wait while he was on the continent involved in ecclesiastical business.

Catherine had taught others to accept this type of situation as greater mortification than rigorous fasting or other bodily penances. Having issued an invitation that proceeded from a sense of hospitality, she felt responsible for the ensuing sense of excitement that the acceptance created. She carried the burden of the disappointment that would befall all concerned if the event did not transpire, and seemed a little put out with herself that she had let the word get out before she received confirmation of the date of the arrival of the English bishop.

Catherine's immediate correction of her statement demonstrates that she remained a real human being who every day, every hour, chose God anew.

In examining closely the life of one whose constant endeavor was to imitate the pattern laid out by the Gospels, the flaws which exist indicate the depth and reality of the surrender to the call of Jesus. Without the flaws, the struggle, the pain, the dying daily might well be missed. Evidence in confidential letters to Frances Warde reveals where Catherine McAuley experienced her own need for mercy. Hers was not a holiness that effaced the "human."

Among Catherine's friends, Frances Warde, who had served as her confidential secretary and business manager in the early days of Baggot Street, held special place. The first to be professed by Catherine, Frances was friend, confidant, partner in aspiration and enterprise, and co-foundress in Carlow. To Frances, Catherine wrote her most unguarded remarks.

Energized by friendship, that choicest of all human gifts, Catherine looked forward to visits to friends as a comfort to herself, a comfort she envisioned gratefully. Feeling the need of a friend's deep understanding, she did not hesitate to acknowledge her appreciation for the solace of friendship.

> The prospect of my visit to Limerick will animate me. I need scarcely tell you that it will be a source of great happiness, for which I thank God, a pure, heartfelt friendship which renews the powers of mind and body.[216]

Away from Baggot Street on foundation travels, Catherine carried pressing concerns for those she had left, especially for Sister dePazzi Delaney. Nagging concern that imprudent overindulgence in prayer, fasting, or works would upset dePazzi's health or her disposition recurred in Catherine's confidential letters. Sister de Pazzi, the assistant who presided in her absence, was subject to epileptic attacks and gave Catherine many difficult days.

This sister's manifest gloom at the departure of the two Baggot Street sisters whom Catherine had lent to assist in Bermondsey, added to Catherine's burden. Handling that little cross with her own advice to "notice the faults of every day but often in a playful way," Catherine wrote:

> Mother de Pazzi and I have kept up a regular concert of sighing and moaning since the Sisters went, but this day I was resolved not to be outdone, or even equalled, so commenced groaning for every sigh she gave, and our sorrows have ended in laughing at each other.[217]

The rub and force of these pressures created the glow of Catherine's compassion. That she felt the rub is clear from the passing allusions in her letters.

Catherine's impatience with Clare Augustine Moore's artistic temperament, for example, was long-standing. Whether in comments on Clare Augustine's artistic judgment or her strong will, Catherine's inability to understand this sister is clear. Earlier she had dubbed her the *Judge*, commenting:

> I do not mind half what she says on these scientific points, which she delights in unfolding to the fools that will hearken to her. She will do anything in the Register you wish, but what is mentioned, she calls three weeks work... she is very slow.[218]
>
> *That one* has more of her own ways yet than ours. And it is not very easy to fix her to a point. She finds the duties sufficient to fill up her time, and as her constitution is strong, she is much employed in outdoor work.[219]

Clare Augustine visited the sick poor and did whatever else constituted outdoor work. Whatever the substance of Catherine McAuley's fashionably proper education, it evidently did not include Ireland's most famous art work—lettering and illumination. Her candid comments reveal clearly that she lacked appreciation for the skill, the time, and the talent involved, and found the temperament of the artist uncongenial. In another letter she confided to Frances:

Sister Mary Clare Moore is a character, not suited to my taste or my ability to govern, though possessing many very estimable points. She teased and perplexed me so much about the difficulty of copying the two pages, that I was really obliged to give up, unwilling to command lest it should produce disedifying consequences. She said it would take the entire Lent. Indeed, you can have no idea how little she does in a week. As to a day's work, it is laughable to look at it. She will show me 3 leaves, saying, "I fined these today." 3 rose or lilly [sic] leaves.[220]

Generous enough to locate much of the difficulty of this relationship within herself, Catherine knew how unproductive is solving one's own lack of virtue by reforming someone else. Putting forth the challenge of taking up the cross daily, she had queried: "How does [a religious] expect to take up her cross and follow Christ if she is not to find it in her associates?" It is significant that, despite the exasperation she experienced, so disciplined was her control of herself and so habitual were the little deaths of self transcendance, that Clare Augustine would record in her Memoir: "She liked to look at me drawing or working."[221]

Chapter XII

LEGACY AND CHALLENGE OF CATHERINE MCAULEY

When Catherine McAuley was asked to provide an account of her Institute of Mercy from its inception, she demurred that she "would find it most difficult ... [since] the circumstances which would make it interesting could never be introduced in public discourse."[222] It was only in candid letters to her community that the private details of joy and sorrow, enthusiasm and discouragement, pain, humiliation, and struggle emerged.

However, acknowledging that she was omitting all that might engage attention, she responded with a circumspect account attributing to God's providence and to the guidance of the clergy who advised her whatever progress had occurred.

It commenced with 2, Sister Doyle and I. The plan from the beginning was such as is now in practice. In '27 the House was opened. In a year and a half we were joined so fast that it became a matter of general wonder. Doctor Murray gave his most cordial approbation and visited frequently. All was done under his direction from the time we entered the House, which was erected for the purpose of Charity.

Doctor Blake and Rev. Armstrong were chiefly concerned, received all the ideas I had formed, and consulted for 2 years at least before the House was built. I am sure Doctor Blake had it constantly before him in all his communications with Heaven, for I never can forget his fervent prayers when it was in progress.

Seeing us increase so rapidly, and all going on in the greatest order almost of itself, great anxiety was expressed to give it stability. We who began were prepared to do whatever was recommended and in September 1830, we went with dear Sister Harley to George's Hill to serve a novitiate for the purpose of firmly establishing it. In December '31 we returned and the progress has gone on as you know. We have now gone beyond 100 in number, and the desire to join seems rather to increase, though it was thought the foundations would retard it.[223]

Catherine's evaluation of all that had happened underscored her deep faith as well as her lack of self-congratulation. She had accepted the advice she sought; she had done as she was bidden; she had experienced a providential guidance despite the want of "prudence, vigilance, or judgment."

From her understanding of Jesus' pressing invitation to follow him in living life in the Father through willing acceptance of the mystery of his love, whether manifested in peace and joy, in pain and suffering, or even in death, Catherine McAuley deepened her response to whomever she met, to whatever she experienced, and to the movements of her own heart and soul.

Over and over, her letters sought to knead the spirit of union and charity through the dough of the expanding institute. When she sent word from Birr that they laughed at their hardships—among them oatmeal so frozen it broke one's tooth, butter so hard it was necessary to keep hot turf under it in order to cut it, and she herself, petrified with cold and feeling the frost most acutely in her right side from hip to ankle—and danced every night, she declared indirectly that their mutual sharing of good things and bad was building the bond of perfection, union, and charity, among them.

The spontaneous character of Catherine's letter writing permitted her to dot the letters with bulletins concerning her own health. Sometimes she spoke of her pains and aches to explain why she had to omit or delay some particular action. Other times, she recorded what she felt as she wrote. Her essential incorporation of pain and suffering as the reality of life turned most of her admissions into a trusting acceptance of whatever God permitted.

Almost clinical in describing her ailments, Catherine usually identified her illness, gave progress reports, and included any complications that developed. While she neither hid from herself or others that she had an affliction, she refused to bemoan it. Seeking neither sympathy nor service, she merely accepted her limitations as evident in her message to Frances Warde:

> As to my delay in writing, I have been tortured with my unfortunate mouth, only just getting a little better, and in the midst of other matters, the Limerick Foundation was prepared and concluded for the first week in September.[224]

In another comment to Frances after the London foundation, she registered the toll that foundation making took on her.

> I have been chiefly confined to bed since my return—not down until yesterday. First an affection of my stomach, etc. for which I was obliged to have a physician, and then my old mouth complaint, to a great degree, which has kept me on Infant's diet more than ten days.[225]

Arriving at Limerick after a difficult stop at troubled Charleville and happier ones at Tullamore and Cork, she telescoped the personal cost of the constant demands of newness—meeting new persons, new customs, new surroundings, new expectations—in one descriptive word to Teresa White.

> There is a most simple, inviting tomb just opposite the cell I occupy. A holy abbess and a lay sister are deposited there.[226]

"Inviting" recorded something of the weariness affecting her, and revealed the extent to which her life-long fear of death had evaporated.

In a later letter, she confessed to Elizabeth Moore that she had to be realistic about how much travel she could demand of her failing strength:

...who am journeying fast enough out of this miserable world. Every day I am weak at some time. My stomach has never recovered its last attack—frequent swellings and soreness.[227]

That travel tormented her more and more as foundations rapidly succeeded one another hinted at her deteriorating health. Beginning to speak more often of her discomfort in her letters, she exclaimed to Frances Warde upon her return from Galway:

On this last occasion I travelled one hundred miles a day, which is very fatiguing except on railways...[228]

Sick, weary, and in physical pain, Catherine felt the burden of long journeys. In letters from Birr, the last foundation she made in Ireland, waiting tasks seemed to cause her to reflect on the absence of those first companions, intensifying her affection for them. Whether the cold of Birr had affected her with new pain or whether she was suffering more severely from chronic illness than she admitted, Catherine was nostalgic about her first companions.

I will not expect a letter from you when I return to our old dear habitation, where I shall never again see all my dearly beloved Sisters—all strange faces. They say that the first separation from kindred, etc. was a joyful sorrow, but that the separations in religion are bitter sorrows. What must it be to me who never met an unkind Sister yet.[229]

Commenting "This is a gloomy subject," she seemed to underscore her lonesomeness for those first devoted and understanding companions whom she had surrendered to the needs of other towns in Ireland and England. To sustain deep pain of loss, Catherine drew upon her faith in the promises of Jesus: "Will we all meet in heaven? Oh what joy, even to think of it."

Catherine usually spoke even of her illnesses in such playful, disarming language that the sisters were encouraged to assume her infirmities were minor complaints. To Teresa White in Galway she sent a health bulletin more to be enjoyed than to admit failing health.

> I have a real old man's cough—old woman's is entirely exploded from the new fashionable vocabulary—no such character is to be recognized in the future.[230]

Telling Cecilia Marmion from Birr that she was stiff and sore, she made light of what, in retrospect, was an increasing burden.

> I feel the frost most acutely in my right side from my hip to my ankle. I have put on a great flannel bandage with camphorated spirit, and trust in God it will, like a dear good old acquaintance, carry me safe back.[231]

For her own illnesses, she preferred to diagnose and prescribe her remedies. She either was wary of being confined by physicians to a lengthy stay as a bedridden patient or she had enough experience with the sick to judge doctoring herself sufficient.

Recognizing in Birmingham the seriousness of her own physical condition, Catherine wrote to arrange for the care she would need. But while she gave specific details to Teresa Carton for a new bed, she thought too of Teresa's needs. This lay sister, who had charge of household affairs, devoted herself to caring for Catherine.

> I am going to give you some cautions {and commissions. Mother de Pazzi tells me the parlours are coloring. I hope you will be careful} not to get a fresh cold. Do not go to sit in the room until it is perfectly dry. I hope the chimneys of both were well swept before the ceilings were whitened.
> {Bespeak an iron bedstead wherever you can get it made in one week. The directions are as follows}:[232]

While Teresa no doubt cut off the directions to give the bed maker, the record of how emphatic Catherine was that no one change her specifications remained. She felt she knew what she needed.

> You will try to have it done exactly. Make the person read it well. He will think the bed too near the ground, but it is to be so. ... Move your bed in where Sr. M. Clare's is and clear out your corner for mine, where I will not hear the noise of the street. I will want a fire. ... You are not to leave the room, a little coughing will never disturb me. I am much better there. Some days very bad appetite. I do not like the bread or butter. It is quite different. Do not have any hurry about getting the bed done. It will be time enough—the third bed to be taken away. It is strange to me, my dear Sister Teresa, to write so much about myself and to give such trouble.[233]

Catherine left a record both of the practical requirements of illness and her embarrassment to focus so strongly on her own needs. The letter is distracted and fluctuates between her personal wishes and consideration for another.

Even when fatal illness loomed, it failed to rob her of amusement at the doctor's direction that her "servant" apply a liniment to her chest.

> Mother de P. has got that appointment. I call every night for my servant. ... I am sure her Majesty is not attended with half so much care, often ungraciously received by a poor, unfortunate peevish old sinner, who never required any particular care or attention before, and who is more weary of it than of the delicacy that occasions it.[234]

Discovering it took much psychic energy to cope well with smothering attentiveness from "kind tormentors,"[235] she nevertheless appreciated the goodness demonstrated. For those who wanted to do more than she could absorb, she had her own defense.

> ...to the affectionate, often—repeated question: "Rev. Mother, what could you take?" the best

answer is: "My heart you tease me very much."[236]

As she communicated her condition, she confused the issue by explaining that it was Father O'Hanlon, not the doctor, who had put her under bedrest restraint.

> I should add that it was not the Doctor desired me not to read, etc., it was Father O'Hanlon. The Doctor in a melancholy tone left me to my own wishes. I might take anything I liked. He seemed evidently to regard the case as hopeless.[237]

Having acquiesced to the visit from the doctor at her ecclesiastical superior's urging, Catherine persisted in making light of her illness, advancing her own theories about the state of her health:

> As we should carefully examine the motive of our action, I here humbly confess that my chief motive, just now is to show that one of the most distinguished amongst our medical profession may be mistaken and that we should not immediately take up their opinions.[238]

Early in October, Catherine concluded her last letter to Sister Juliana Hardman in Birmingham with an assurance that she had picked up strength,

> I kept for the last what I know you will like to hear, that every person who has seen me since my return thinks I look much better.[239]

In a final letter to Birr, Catherine was cryptic regarding her health, following an assertion of strength with a request for prayers for a happy death. She trusted Aloysius' prudence not to sound an alarm throughout the institute as some might have done.

> Pray, who gave you such a false account of me. I am just as you saw me. Pray fervently that God may grant me the grace of a holy, penitential preparation, and the grace of a happy death.[240]

Gifts of nature and grace had permitted Catherine McAuley, in only ten years as a Sister of Mercy, to be many things: an evangelist in Charleville where one ancient cooed, "Sure it was the Lord who drove you in amongst us"; a pioneer in Carlow, where no one had thought to provide furniture for the convent and where a pension (tuition) school was introduced for the new middle class; a diplomat in Cork, where the bishop kept close watch on admissions; an incorporator in Limerick, where she received two Poor Clare nuns whose convent had failed; an apologist in Birr, where a schism had depleted the parish; and an ambassador in the English foundations at Bermondsey and Birmingham; as well as home visitor in Tullamore and Galway—all works which had their roots in the house on Baggot Street.

The extant letters begin with a request for the collection of interest due on a bond and end with a request to collect a small legacy. Thus the good steward closed her earthly accounts to begin the process of yielding an open heart and a detached spirit to her God.

Saving the doctor who attended her final illness from any sense of discomfiture, Catherine forestalled his prognosis with the quiet comment that "the scene is drawing to a close."[241] But before the end, the fond affection in which she had held her community bade her speak to each of those at Baggot Street individually. In the midst of special messages to each, "her first and last injunction to all was to preserve union and peace amongst [them],"[242] her dying exhortation to her community that they love one another.

Attentive to the fatigue experienced by those surrounding her deathbed, she who had urged her sisters to vie with one another with "tender concern and regard," died as she had lived, modeling such behavior with the thoughtful whisper to one of the sisters to "be sure to have a comfortable cup of tea for them when I am gone."[243]

Catherine knew Jesus as Christ the Lord but she also knew him as Jesus of Nazareth, the Son who had truly put on human life who was able to be imitated, who called the human family to live his way of Mercy, of courageous service in truth and justice, and of forgiveness gentled by love and open to the gift of those served.

If Catherine had lived at the end of the twentieth century, instead of the cry of the poor children of Dublin haunting her dreams, the cries of a suffering world would have troubled her sleep. She would no doubt have turned her energy to global interrelationships of rich and poor, knowing that as long as in any country the poor, the sick, the uneducated are oppressed or marginated, the light of the Gospels is dimmed and peace and justice in the world remain elusive ideals.

In the contemporary world, in spite of energetic measures to alleviate the ills of society—poverty, sickness, ignorance—the poor, the sick, the ignorant abound; the alienated, the lonely, the deserted, and the abused abound.

In a world of indifference concerning belief, the erosion of faith in God and in transcendent reality has spawned self-destructive greed, selfishness, and life styles of out-maneuvering one another. Out of the consequent erosion of integrity in word and work, dishonesty, brutality, and destructiveness abound.

When were spiritual and temporal works of mercy—performed with tender courage—more needed? In her day, Catherine found her response—misericordia. She brought her heart to misery and in the self-gift released a call still heard. By courageous, contagious concern for the spiritual and temporal welfare of the poor, the sick, and the ignorant, she broke through the impossibilities of her time. She animated many to walk with her. She animated others at centers of wealth, power, and influence to share in her heroic efforts. She connected the rich to the poor, the healthy to the sick, the educated and skilled to the uninstructed, the influential to those of no consequence, the powerful to the weak to do the work of God on earth.

Endnotes

1. Sister Mary Ignatia Neumann, RSM, ed., *Letters of Catherine McAuley* (Baltimore: Helicon Press, 1969) contains 177 of these letters.

2. Thomas H. Johnson, ed., *The Poems of Emily Dickinson* (Cambridge, Massachusetts: The Belknap Press, 1977), II, #989, p.715.

3. In the absence of any records of Catherine McAuley's birth, early biographers give conflicting dates. It is now clear from the probate of her father's will in 1783 that the 1787 date inscribed on her tombstone is in error. Since 1778 is the date given by both Sr. Vincent Hartnett, a novice trained by Catherine McAuley, and the writer of the Annals of the Tullamore convent where Catherine's earliest associate, Mary Anne Doyle was the superior, some conjecture that the engraver may have transposed the two final digits. The Irish Postal Service issued a stamp commemorating the 200th anniversary of the birth of Catherine McAuley in 1978.

4. James McGauley married Elinor Conway. After his death she dropped the G in McGauley. The three children of this marriage—Catherine, Mary, and James—spelled their name McAuley in imitation of their mother, although later in his life, James adopted the fashionable Protestant spelling of his name, Macauley.

5. The Penal Codes perpetuated a racial division upon religious grounds and ensured the political, social, and to an extent economic, ascendency of a small minority whose privilege included a monopoly of higher education.

6. Although Anglo-Irish is essentially a historian's term, it refers to those who shared neither the religion nor the ethnic origin of the Catholic majority in Ireland.

7. Bermondsey Annals, photocopy, p.28.

8. Well-educated men of three hitherto mutually exclusive groups developed an organization known as the United Irishmen which grew apace with Catherine's adolescence. It brought together Anglo-Irish Protestants, Scots- Presbyterians, and Irish Roman Catholics. These patriots tabled religious differences to seek Ireland's political independence from England. Their efforts came to nothing. By 1798, uprisings in Belfast, Wexford, and Limerick were separately smashed. The Irish Parliament voted itself out of existence in 1800, its members to sit thenceforth in the Parliament of England.

9. Leases cited by Sister M. Bertrand Degnan, RSM, *Mercy Unto Thousands* (Westminster, Maryland: The Newman Press, 1957), p. 351.

10. Apothecaries Hall was a training school for doctors, midwives, and pharmacists, built in 1790 as a result of the Irish Apothecaries Act. Original members had to swear an oath against the doctrine of Transubstantiation, clear evidence of the Protestant climate.

11. Sister M. Monica O'Doherty, *Memoir of Mother M. Catherine McAuley*, p.5. Photocopy of illuminated manuscript held by the Sisters of Mercy, Silver Spring, Md. Sister Monica was a novice at the time of Catherine McAuley's death.

12. Religion was not a private matter. The Ascendency, of which the Armstrongs were members, comprised descendants of families planted earlier in Ireland by Henry VIII and Elizabeth I to be loyal subjects of the English crown, adhering to the Anglican Church and accepting the king as its head. These immigrants were awarded lands confiscated from Roman Catholic Irish, the lands becoming known as the Pale. While much of the geography of the Pale comprised the area around Dublin,it also contained magnificent estates throughout Ireland. Privilege established by law gave Ascendency landlords absolute rights over their holdings. They could evict without notice, establish punishing rents, demand the best from harvests, levy taxes on improvements made by the tenant. Holding

all legislative, executive, and judicial posts, they were reluctant to seat non-conforming Protestants in Parliament, and even more reluctant to seat Roman Catholics. When Catherine is described as living in a Roman Catholic household, she is described as living within limited boundaries socially and politically. But when she is described as joining a Protestant household, she is described as entering an ambience of privilege where few of the privileges pertained to her.

13. The Act of Union (1800), an attempt by the British government to impose a political solution once and for all upon the ills that plagued Ireland, resulted in the departure of a large segment of the intellectual and economic elite from Dublin to London. This exodus caused economic ruin to those industries and businesses which depended on a thriving metropolis.

14. Throughout Catherine's development as a mature Christian, she had the direction of learned and holy priests. Dean Lube, and Rev. Thomas Betagh, SJ, were early mentors. Rev. Edward Armstrong and Dr. Michael Blake, later bishop of Dromore, were loyal friends, wise advisors, and eloquent advocates of the House of Mercy.

15. Her confidants, Dr. Michael Blake and Dr. William Armstrong, administrator of St. Andrew parish, Westland Row, encouraged her to build the house in a prominent section of Dublin near Merrion Square where the poor could be seen in their reality by the wealthy of the neighborhood. The section chosen was a property leased for 150 years from the Pembrook estate on Lower Baggot Street. Leases for 150 years were virtually considered purchases and provided a legal bypass of the proscription of Roman Catholic ownership. This property was within the confines of St. Andrew parish and it was no doubt appealing to Catherine to be a member since Dr. Armstrong had become one of her most trusted advisors as well as her confessor. Dr. Daniel Murray, archbishop of Dublin, gave his official approval to each new development.

16. Awarded in pounds sterling, her £24,000 inheritance might well translate in late twentieth century inflationary economy to more than $1,000,000. For some further un-

derstanding of the amounts involved, between 1800 and 1845, day laborers were paid 4 to 8 pence per day. (U.S. translation: $.25 to $.75 per day.)

17. S.J. Connolly in *Priests and People in Pre-Famine Ireland* (New York: St. Martin's Press, 1982), p.83 notes that diocesan statutes obliged parish priests to provide religious instruction of the young through the establishment of catechism classes. The instruction provided at these classes was not usually given by the clergy themselves, but by suitable lay persons recruited for the purpose.

18. ibid., p.75, states that the years between 1820 and 1860 were the period of the "Second Reformation" when a whole range of dedicated and well-supported Protestant societies devoted themselves to the task of the conversion of the Catholic Irish.

19. Derry L Ms., unpublished. Internal evidence indicates it is the work of someone serving as personal secretary to Sr. Mary Anne Doyle, first associate of Catherine McAuley. Typescript copy is located in archives of Sisters of Mercy, Silver Spring, Md.

20. Ibid.

21. Ibid.

22. Dublin Ms., unpublished memoir of Sister M. Clare Augustine Moore.

23. Sister Mary Ignatia Neumann, RSM, ed., *Letters of Catherine McAuley*, op. cit., p.69, September 10, 1828. Subsequent references to this volume will be cited as *Letters*.

24. Dublin Ms.

25. Roland Burke Savage, S.J., *Catherine McAuley* (Dublin: M.H. Gill and Son, Ltd., 1955), p. 102.

26. Dublin Ms.

27. A long-outdated code of canon law contained no provisions for communities of vowed women who were not enclosed. Such groups were explicitly condemned under a still-operative Bull issued by Pope Pius V in 1566, a status regularized only in 1900 by Leo XIII.

28. Dublin Ms.

29. Quote attributed to Archbishop Murray in unpublished Annals of Bermondsey foundation. Photocopy available in archives of Sisters of Mercy, Silver Spring, Md.

30. *Letters*, p.69, September 10, 1828.

31. Dublin Ms.

32. *Letters*, p. 154, January 13, 1839.

33. *Letters*, p.81, December 13, 1836.

34. *Letters*, p.273. Catherine's teasing reference to the superiors of the various foundations.

35. While the documents of Vatican II, particularly *Perfectae Caritatis,* recommended that all religious families return to the authentic sources from which their life derives, the spirit of the founder, the term "charism" was not used with reference to religious life until paul VI's Apostolic Exhortation on Renewal of Religious Life, *Evangelica Testificatio.*

36. *Letters*, p.216, June 6, 1840.

37. Bermondsey Annals.

38. *Letters*, p.141, October 25, 1838.

39. *Letters*, p.284, January 2 or 3, 1841.

40. *Letters*, p.289, January 4, 1841.

41. *Letters*, p.286, January 2 or 3, 1841.

42. *Letters*, p.291, January 15, 1841.

43. *Letters*, p.132, August 23, 1838.

44. *Letters*, p.140, October 25, 1838.

45. Ibid.

46. *Letters*, p.144, November 15, 1838.

47. *Letters*, p.95, August 1837.

48. Ibid.

49. *Letters*, p.126, May 15, 1838.

50. *Letters*, p.228, July 30, 1840.

51. Unpublished letter to Sister M. Vincent Hartnett, November, 1840. Copy located in Carysfort Archives.

52. *Letters*, p.216, June 6, 1840.

53. *Letters*, p.292, January 15, 1841.

54. Lay communities—ipso facto, religious—had to have an "ecclesiastical superior" who was responsible for approving the acquisition of property, the undertaking of new ministries, fund-raising, travel, admission of members, and the election of superiors.

55. *Letters*, p.242-43, October 26, 1840.

56. Ibid.

57. *Letters*, p.215, June 6, 1840.

58. Ibid.

59. Ibid.

60. *Letters*, p.245, October 28, 1840.

61. Ibid.

62. Unpublished segment of the letter of October 4, 1837, published in *Letters*, pp.97-99. Underlined em-

phasis is Catherine McAuley's. This segment was found among papers in the Bermondsey archives by Sister M. Hermenia, RSM, while involved in research for a biography of Sister M. Austin Carroll.

63. *Letters*, p.319, March 28, 1841.

64. *Letters*, p.301-02, February 3, 1841.

65. *Letters*, p.290, early in 1841.

66. *Letters*, p.152, January 7, 1839.

67. Ibid.

68. Derry L Ms.

69. Dublin Ms.

70. Ibid.

71. Unpublished fragment, dated March 13, 1838; located in archives of Sisters of Mercy, Silver Spring, Md.

72. *Freeman's Journal*, April 6, 1830.

73. *Letters*, p.74, December 2, 1835.

74. Unpublished letter of February 29, 1840. Located in Carysfort archives.

75. *Letters*, p.117, January 29, 1838.

76. *Letters*, p.114, January 10, 1838.

77. *Letters*, p.123, April 25, 1838.

78. *Letters*, p.126, May 15, 1838.

79. *Letters*, p.127, May 15, 1838.

80. *Letters*, p.122, April 9, 1838.

81. *Letters*, p.176, November 15, 1839.

82. *Letters*, p.199, February 26, 1840.

83. Sister M. Teresa Austin Carroll, RSM, *Life of Catherine McAuley*, (St. Louis: The Vincentian Press, 1893), p.242.

84. Dublin Ms.

85. *Letters*, p.87, June 27, 1837.

86. Bishop Donnelly, *A Short History of Some Dublin Parishes* (Dublin: Catholic Truth Society, 1907), p.161. Cited in Sister M. Bertrand Degnan, RSM, *Mercy Unto Thousands* (Westminster, Maryland: The Newman Press, 1957), p.170.

87. *Letters*, p.376, September 24, 1841.

88. *Letters*, p.241, October 18, 1840.

89. *Letters*, p.241, October 18, 1840.

90. *Letters*, p.225, July 25, 1840.

91. The Derry Ms. comments with reference to the admission of "lay" members that four were admitted and "placed much on the same footing as those destined for choir nuns, eat at same table, passed time of recreation with them, etc. This, it was soon found, would not answer."
    Further discussion of the class-consciousness which "ran through all levels of Irish society in this period" may be found in S. J. Connolly, *Priests and People in Pre-Famine Ireland*, (New York: St. Martin's Press, 1982), esp. pp. 29- 32.

92. Unpublished letter to Frances Warde dated February 1839. Original is located in archives, Sisters of Mercy, Windham.

93. *Letters*, p.194, January 18, 1840.

94. *Letters*, p.348, July 19, 1841.

95. *Letters*, p.151, January 7, 1839.

96. *Letters*, p.376, September 24, 1841.

97. Ibid.

98. *Letters*, p.353, July 24, 1841.

99. Ibid.

100. *Letters*, p.93, July 27, 1837. Emphasis mine.

101. *Letters*, p.327, April 6, 1841.

102. *Letters*, p.106, December 20, 1837.

103. Ibid.

104. *Letters*, p.107, December 20, 1837.

105. Ibid.

106. Ibid.

107. *Letters*, p.138, October 12, 1838.

108. The population grew, for example, from 4,900,000 in 1800 to 8,175,000 in 1841.Cited by Emmet Larkin in "The Devotional Revolution in Ireland," *American Historical Review*, 77 (June 1972), p.636.

109. Photocopy of original handwritten prayer located in the archives of the Sisters of Mercy, Burlingame, Ca. Emphasis mine.

110. *Letters*, p.260, December 7, 1840.

111. *Letters*, pp.342, 129, 272.

112. *Letters*, p.293, January 15, 1841.

113. *Letters*, p.347, June 30, 1841.

114. *Letters*, p.256, November 24, 1840.

115. *Letters*, p.313, March 5, 1841.

116. *Letters*, p.147, November 17, 1838.

117. Ibid.

118. *Letters*, p.80, September 5, 1836.

119. *Letters*, p.197, February 4, 1840.

120. *Letters*, p.249, November 6, 1840.

121. *Letters*, p.257-58, November 30, 1840.

122. *Letters*, p.258, November 30, 1840.

123. *Letters*, p.254, November 17, 1840.

124. Unpublished verse addressed to Sister M. Ursula Frayne.

125. *Letters*, p.313, March 11, 1841.

126. *Letters*, p.151, January 7, 1839.

127. *Letters*, p.88, July 1, 1837.

128. Savage, op cit., p.150. Savage also states that at the height of the plague, deaths in Dublin averaged over 600 a day.

129. *Letters*, p.129, June 16, 1838.

130. Original Rule in Catherine McAuley's handwriting.

131. *Letters*, p.340, May 25, 1841.

132. *Letters*, p.286, January 2 or 3, 1841.

133. *Letters*, p.232, August 20, 1840.

134. Sister M. Angela Bolster, "Catherine McAuley, Her Educational Thought and Its Influence," unpublished paper. Sister Angela also notes that a period of three years as monitress in an approved teaching establishment was required in order to secure a teacher's certificate according to the regulations of the Board of Education.

135. Rules and Constitutions of the Presentation Sisters, 1809. Chapter 1, #5.

136. Carlow Annals for 1840, p.38. Although Carlow is generally recognized as having established the first "pension school," the Derry L manuscript compiled by Catherine McAuley's earliest associate, Mary Anne Doyle, notes that in the spring of 1830, before the Institute of Mercy was formally established, "a school for young ladies was opened in the refectory [At Baggot Street]; but it proved a signal failure and the very few pupils it ever contained dropped off within the year."

137. *Letters*, p.173, October 18, 1839.

138. *Letters*, p.253, November 13, 1840.

139. *Letters*, p.322, March 29, 1841.

140. Obituary of Catherine McAuley, published in *Halifax Register*. Quoted in *Life of Catherine McAuley*, written by a member or the Order of Mercy, with an Introduction by The Venerable Richard Baptist O'Brien [The priest assigned to Nova Scotia in 1838] (P.J.Kenedy and Sons, New York, 1870), pp.445-47.

141. *Life of Catherine McAuley* with Introduction by Rev. Richard O'Brien, p.33. op.cit.

142. *Letters*, p.325, March or April, 1841.

143. *Letters*, p.346, June 30, 1841.

144. Ibid.

145. *The Times*, London, September 9, 1839, p.5; January 8, 1840, p.7.

146. Unpublished addendum to letter fragment published in *Letters*, p.176- 77.

147. *Letters*, p.185, December 17, 1839.

148. Ibid.

149. Ibid.

150. Unpublished letter of Catherine McAuley to Elizabeth Moore, February 29, 1840. Handwritten copies of this letter are located in the archives of Carysfort and Cork.

151. *Letters*, p.378, September 25, 1841.

152. Ibid.

153. Ibid.

154. *Letters*, p.189, December 26, 1839. Architect also for the second Convent of Mercy in England, Pugin accommodated some of Catherine's wishes at Birmingham. He brought the windows to eye level and provided more places for light to enter. Bermondsey Convent was destroyed in World War II. Birmingham's survived and is now registered as a national historic building.

155. *Letters*, p.189, December 17, 1839.

156. *Letters*, p.174, November 13, 1839. Letter to Dr. Francis Haly, bishop of Kildare and Leighlin.

157. *Letters*, p.238, October 14, 1840.

158. Ibid.

159. *Letters*, p.155, January 13, 1839.

160. *Letters*, p.272, December 17, 1840.

161. *Letters*, p.360, August 1841.

162. *Letters*, p.81, December 13, 1836.

163. *Letters*, p.330-31, Easter Monday, 1841.

164. *Letters*, p.79, July 2, 1836.

165. *Letters*, p.226, July 28, 1840.

166. *Letters*, p.79, July 2, 1836.

167. *Letters*, p.274, December 20, 1840. Translation of Gaelic phrase: "A hundred thousand welcomes."

168. *Retreat Instructions*, compiled by Sister M. Teresa Purcell, Dublin and Tullamore, and edited by Sisters of Mercy, Albany, N.Y. (The Newman Press; Westminster, Maryland, 1952), p.114.

169. *Letters*, p.163, May 11, 1839.

170. *Letters*, p.310, February 28, 1841.

171. *Bermondsey Manuscript*, a treatise known as "The Spirit of the Institute." Although the original was destroyed during World War II, a typed copy has been preserved in the archives of Carysfort Convent, Ireland, and a photostat of this is available in the archives, Sisters of Mercy, Silver Spring, MD. It is reproduced in *Letters of Catherine McAuley*, pp.385-91.

172. *Retreat Instructions*, p.154.

173. *Letters*, p.273, December 20, 1840.

174. Dublin Ms.

175. Ibid.

176. Derry L Ms.

177. Dublin Ms.

178. Carlow Annals, pp.25-26.

179. Bermondsey Annals, p.45.

180. Tullamore Annals, p.9, quoting unpublished letter of Catherine McAuley.

181. Carlow Annals, p.43.

182. *Retreat Instructions*, p.162.

183. *Letters*, p.312, March 5, 1841.

184. Dublin Ms.

185. *Letters*, p.35, July 26, 1841. Emphasis is found on original letter in Catherine McAuley's handwriting.

186. Bermondsey Annals, p.99.

187. Named superior at the Bermondsey Convent of Mercy on Sr. M. Clare Moore's return to Ireland, Elizabeth Agnew (Sr. M.Clare), unsuccessful in her efforts to have the Rule changed to permit contemplative life, left Bermondsey to join the community at La Trappe.

Not finding the Trappistine life to her liking, she made several unavailing efforts to be re-admitted to the Sisters of Mercy.

A prominent convert, widely known for her successful novel, *Geraldine*, Miss Agnew had the support of several members of the hierarchy in subsequent ventures to found both a convent in Rome which failed, and another in London which also disbanded. She lived out a long life writing novels in Italy.

188. *Bermondsey Manuscript*, op. cit.

189. *Letters*, p.131, July 3, 1838.

190. *Letters*, p.204, March 21, 1840.

191. Unpublished letter to Dr. Hamilton, *Hamilton Papers*, December 19, 1837. Located in archives, archbishop's residence, Drumcondra, Ireland.

192. *Letters*, p.115, January 17, 1838.

193. Savage, op.cit., p.227.

194. *Letters*, p.115, January 17, 1838.

195. *Letters*, p.102, November 22, 1837.

196. *Hamilton Papers*, dated December 19, 1837.

197. Savage, p.227.

198. *Hamilton Papers*, dated only 1838.

199. *Letters*, p.166, July 24, 1839.

200. *Letters*, p.129, June 16, 1838.

201. *Letters*, p.102-03, November 22, 1837.

202. *Letters*, p.125, May 15, 1838.

203. *Letters*, p.116, January 17, 1838.

204. *Letters*, p.142, November 1, 1838.

205. Ibid.

206. *Letters*, p.204, March 21, 1840.

207. *Letters*, p.125, May 15, 1838.

208. *Letters*, p.94, August 8, 1837.

209. *Letters*, p.127-28, June 16, 1838.

210. *Letters*, p.118, February, 17, 1838.

211. Ibid.

212. *Letters*, p.341, May 28, 1841.

213. Ibid.

214. Ibid.

215. *Letters*, p.356, July 31, 1841.

216. *Letters*, p.206, March 24, 1840.

217. *Letters*, p.242, October 18, 1840.

218. *Letters*, p.158, January 22 and 25, 1839.

219. *Letters*, p.321, March 29, 1841. Emphasis is Catherine McAuley's.

220. *Letters*, p.311-12, March 5, 1841.

221. Dublin Ms.

222. *Letters*, p.154, January 13, 1839.

223. Ibid., pp.154-55.

224. *Letters*, p.132, August 23, 1838.

225. *Letters*, p.195, January 30, 1840.

226. *Letters*, p.137, October 12, 1838.

227. *Letters*, p.202, March 14, 1840.

228. *Letters*, p.238, October 12, 1840.

229. *Letters*, p.304, February 3, 1841.

230. *Letters*, p.222, July 27, 1840.

231. *Letters*, p.305, February 5, 1841.

232. Directions are cut off in original letter. Bracketed segments indicate unpublished sections of letter of September 8, 1841, published in *Letters*, p.373. Original is located in Carysfort archives.

233. *Letters*, p.373, September 8, 1841.

234. *Letters*, p.375, September 20, 1841.

235. *Letters*, p.311, March 5, 1841.

236. *Letters*, p.374, September 20, 1841.

237. Ibid.

238. Ibid.

239. *Letters*, p.380, October 2, 1841.

240. *Letters*, p.381, October 4, 1841.

241. Letter of Elizabeth Moore to Mary Anne Doyle, November 21, 1841.

242. Ibid.

243. Carroll, *Life of Catherine McAuley*, op.cit., p.401.

Bibliography

BOOKS AND PERIODICALS

Bacon, Margaret Hope. *Mothers of Feminism.* San Francisco: Harper & Row, 1986.

Barry, K. M. *Catharine McAuley and the Sisters of Mercy.* Dublin: Fallon and Son, 1894.

Beckett, J.C. *A Short History of Ireland.* London: Hutchinson University Library, 1973.

Bolster, Sister M. Angela, RSM. *Catherine McAuley in Her Own Words.* Dublin: Dublin Diocesan Office for Causes, 1978.

Breault, William, SJ. *The Lady from Dublin.* Boston: Quinlan Press, 1986.

Buckley, Michael J., SJ. "The Charism of Religious Life," *Review for Religious*, 44 (1985), 654-64.

Carroll, Sister M. Teresa Austin. *Leaves from the Annals of the Sisters of Mercy*, 4 vols. New York: P. O'Shea, Publisher, 1881, 1883, 1888, 1895.

Carroll, Sister M. Teresa Austin. *Life of Catherine McAuley.* New York: D. and J. Sadlier and Co., 1866.

Carroll, Sister M. Teresa Austin. *Life of Catherine McAuley.* St. Louis: The Vincentian Press, 1893.

Connolly, S.J. *Priests and People in Pre-Famine Ireland.* New York: Gill and Macmillan, 1982.

Degnan, Sister Mary Bertrand. *Mercy Unto Thousands.* Westminster, Maryland: The Newman Press, 1957.

Evans, Sister M. Daniel, RSM. *From the Letter to the Spirit.* Burlingame: Sisters of Mercy, 1968.

Familiar Instructions of Rev. Mother McAuley. ed. Sisters of Mercy, St. Louis. St. Louis: Carreras, 1888.

George, Francis E., OMI. "Founding Founderology", *Review for Religious,* 36 (1977), 40-48.

Hartnett, Sister M. Vincent. *The Life of Rev. Mother Catherine McAuley.* Dublin: John F. Fowler, 3 Crow St., 1864.

Healy, Kathleen, RSM. *Frances Warde: American Founder of the Sisters of Mercy.* New York: The Seabury Press, 1973.

Irish Spirituality. Ed. Michael Maher. Dublin: Veritas Publications, 1981.

Johnson, Thomas, ed. *The Poems of Emily Dickinson.* 3 vols. Cambridge, Massachusetts: The Belknap Press, 1977.

Lappetito, Sister M. Michael, RSM. *Our Life Together in Mercy: Toward an Apostolic Spirituality.* Burlington, Vermont: Mercy Press, 1980.

Larkin, Emmet. "The Devotional Revolution in Ireland." *American Historical Review,* 77 (June 1972), 625-52.

Lecky, William E.H. *The Leaders of Public Opinion in Ireland.* London: Longmans, Green, and Co., 1871.

Maxwell, Constantia. *Dublin Under the Georges.* Dublin: Hodges Figgis and Co., Ltd., 1946.

McAuley, Catherine. *The Bermondsey Manuscript.* Manuscript on the Spirit of the Sisters of Mercy. Copy located in archives, Sisters of Mercy, Bermondsey, England. Published in *Letters of Catherine McAuley,* ed., Neumann, pp.385- 91.

McAuley, Catherine. *Cottage Controversy.* New York: P. O'Shea, 1883.

McAuley, Catherine. *The Rule of the Sisters of Mercy.* Photostat of original. Burlingame, California: Sisters of Mercy, 1967.

Murphy, Rev. Dominic. "Sisters of Mercy." *Sketches of Irish Nunneries.* Cork: 1865.

Neumann, Sister Mary Ignatia, ed. *Letters of Catherine McAuley.* Baltimore: Helicon Press, Inc., 1969.

O Tuaehaigh, Gearoid. *Ireland Before the Famine: 1798-1848.* Dublin: Gill and Macmillan Ltd., 1972.

Purcell, Sister M. Teresa. *Retreat Instructions of M. M. Catherine McAuley.* Westminster, Md.: Newman Press, 1952.

Quaker Spirituality. Ed. Douglas V. Steere. Rahway: Paulist Press, 1984.

Ryan, E.A., SJ. "The Sisters of Mercy: An Important Chapter in Church History." *Theological Studies,* 18 (June, 1957), 254-70.

Savage, Roland Burke, S.J. *Catherine McAuley: The First Sister of Mercy.* Dublin: M.H. Gill and Son Ltd., 1949.

Tilliard, J.M.R. *There are Charisms and Charisms: The Religious Life.* trans. Olga Prendergast. Lumen Vitae, 1977.

Tocqueville, Alexis de. *Journeys to England and Ireland.* New Haven: Yale University Press, 1958.

Ward, E.C. *The Foundress of the Sisters of Mercy.* Dublin: Sisters of Mercy, 1956.

Woodham-Smith, Cecil. *The Great Hunger: Ireland, 1845-1849.* New York: Harper & Row, 1962.

ANNALS, ARCHIVAL COLLECTIONS, NEWSPAPERS, UNPUBLISHED MANUSCRIPTS

Annals, Archival Collections of Sisters of Mercy:
Ireland: Convents of Mercy—Baggot Street, Birr, Carlow, Carysfort, Charleville, Cork, Galway, Kells, Limerick, Naas, Tullamore, Wexford.
England: Convents of Mercy—Bermondsey, Birmingham.
United States: Federation of the Sisters of Mercy, Chicago, New Hampshire, Pittsburgh.

Bolster, Sister M. Angela, RSM. *Catherine McAuley, Her Educational Thought and Its Influence on the Origin and Development of an Irish Training College.* Unpublished paper.

Derry L Manuscript. *"Notes on the Life of Mother Catherine McAuley"* by a Sister of Mercy. Written Prior to May 15, 1847. Unpublished Manuscript. Archives, Convent of Mercy, Derry, Ireland.

George, Emily, RSM. *The Sisters of Mercy and The Pension School Controversy.* Unpublished paper. February 1981.

Gillgannon, Sister Mary McAuley, RSM. *C. McAuley, Esq.* Unpublished Paper. March 1975.

Greeley, Dolores, RSM. *The Scriptural and Historical Meaning of Compassion.* Unpublished paper. January 1981.

Moore, Sister M. Clare Augustine. *Memoir of the Foundress, M.C. McAuley, 1864.* Unpublished Manuscript. Archives, Sisters of Mercy, Carysfort Park, Dublin.

Rouleau, Sister M. Celeste, RSM. *Authority and Obedience: The Legacy of Catherine McAuley.* Unpublished paper. September 1980.

Sanfilippo, Sister M. Helena, RSM. *Pre-Famine Ireland and the Status of Women.* Unpublished paper in library of Federation of the Sisters of Mercy of the Americas. June 1974.

INDEX